Miss Taken Identity

Come out of the cage and fly into freedom

Loni Hodel

Purpose Publishing

ISBN: 978-1-7337729-7-6

This book is dedicated to everyone who gave me a name:

To Mother and Daddy, for demonstrating the very nature of Father God with your kindness, compassion and love. You honored Him with your sacrifices to make me your daughter – now I want to honor you both with this offering. To Gary, for giving me something even more precious than your last name. You gave me your beautiful heart. To Hope and Grace, for helping me understand what it means to be loved unconditionally. Being your mama is a matchless gift, but to be your best friend is extraordinary.

And, to Jesus, for giving me Your name and because of it, my identity.

TABLE OF CONTENTS

INTRODUCTION

In the early stages of writing this book, I had a dream one night. I realize what I'm about to say might sound strange because we may have never met, but this dream was about *you*. From that night until this very day, Father forever knit you to my heart without me ever knowing your name. I have thought of you often. I've prayed for you to pick up this collective rendering of words that have found their way into chapter after chapter because they were always meant for you.

I dreamt I was at a gathering at a church. The venue was non-descript and unfamiliar, but I knew I was in a place where souls sought solace. I looked up to find the most beautiful young woman I had ever seen coming toward me. With her was a lady I recognized, although not anyone I know in the waking hours. The lady familiar to me was bringing The Beauty to where I was standing – it was as if I was waiting for her. The closer the sweet stranger became, the more I could see: The Beauty's face bore evidence of one who was battered and bruised. She was frightened and fragile, with haunting eyes that held such deep sorrow, I thought I might get lost. Looking at one another, we each knew the other with certain recognition. Immediately moved to compassion, I gently touched her arm. She winced at the pain from her many injuries, and I understood that she was broken both without and within her very being. Even so, she hungrily accepted the gesture of affection, and her wordless expression of gratitude indicated she welcomed hands that were meant to be instruments of healing rather than of harm.

The lady who brought her to me said The Beauty's name was Brandie. Speaking to the woman but looking straight into my eyes through her tortured ones, Brandie softly said, *"She already knows who I am."* The well-meaning woman from church began to explain all the plans she had to help

Brandie with various programs and parties meant to help one in pain. I responded politely that all Brandie needed was to know that she was safe and loved. She needed to know she wasn't alone. She needed someone to take her to Jesus. I knew that someone was me.

It was my weeping that woke me. The pain in The Beauty's face had gripped my heart in such a way that I felt her suffering as if it were my own. It took just a moment before I realized it had been a dream. Then I remembered – before I went to sleep, I prayed that Holy Spirit would speak to me specifically about this book. I had asked Him to reveal even as I slept, whatever *He* wanted me to know. Although His answer wasn't audible, in my spirit, I knew what He was saying – The Beauty in the dream was the reader of this book. I acknowledged this aloud to Him, and then began to pray for *you*. I asked Father to engrave upon my mind Brandie's face and to brand upon my heart the feeling of her suffering. Of *your* suffering.

As I lay in bed praying, Father revealed the meaning behind The Beauty's name. Brandie represents all who are now or have ever, been:

Broken

Ruined

Ashamed

Neglected

Depressed

Insignificant

Empty

If any of these names strike a tender chord within your spirit, it's because this is a divine beckoning to know and believe you are worth fighting for. It is Satan's desire to take from you what Jesus died to give – liberty. It is my intent to expose him for The Thief that he is. This is why you and I are already friends, and why I will address you as such throughout the pages as you read. The words are meant to be instruments of healing for the battered and bruised, frightened and fragile ones haunted by the pain of the past and of the present. I wept the night of the dream because I understood it meant that you have been entrusted to me to assure that you know that you are safe and loved and not alone. I have been called to take you to Jesus and I have taken this calling very seriously. *I already know who you are because I have been you.*

You are so loved that Father made sure your battered and broken heart has been prayed over even before you knew about this book. You are so seen and known by Him that He's shown me your scars and shame in the face of Brandie without me ever seeing yours. You are so valuable, He allowed me to feel the deepest part of sorrow within and without of your being so that I can write for you. That's the kind of God He is – One who woos and pursues and prompts and places us exactly where we need to be. One who will go to great lengths to make Himself known. One who knits hearts and lives together without ever meeting face to face. This book contains portions of my life, but I pray you see yours too, because we're on this sojourn together. This is a delve into deliverance if you'll allow it.

You may not yet realize it yet, Sweetest One, but you've accepted an invitation to freedom.

Chapter One: Ruffled Feathers

"We have something to tell you."

It doesn't matter who you are, where you come from, or what your native tongue happens to be, those words apprehend the air above the room and within your lungs. One declarative sentence encompassing one line and twenty-seven characters will fasten our attention with a vice-like grip until our mind can catch up to where our imagination will inevitably run.

Those six words forever changed my life.

I was between the ages of seven and eight; at the cusp of what experts call the concrete stage of faith development. This is the time a child moves past appreciating religious symbols and rituals, but not yet moving toward the workings of an invisible God. The concrete stage is where the practicality of the things of God begin – church attendance, prayer, and the connection of family to the things of God. This is where a child develops a greater sense of spiritual identity.

And this is where mine was taken.

The new pastor came to visit, not so uncommon in my house, but this time it felt differently. The grown-ups, the ones I knew as my parents, called me into our living room and sat me down. The concern in their faces betrayed their forced smiles, and the heaviness in the room was tangible. Even at seven, I could tell everything was about to change. I listened as my mother explained how my grandmother's sister, the person I'd come to know as a part-time maternal figure, had died. The pastor and my father were silent as she continued, as if they were holding their breath for what came next: somewhere a woman I'd neither known nor heard of was my biological mother. She had "given" me to the woman that had just passed away when she was pregnant with me eight years earlier. I was an unofficial foster child with no past and a questionable future.

I was an unofficial foster child with no past and a questionable future.

The trio in the living room were my constant – one who loved and sacrificed for me, one who protected and provided for me and one who befriended and spoke truth to me, but I was reeling with the news, and everything I thought I knew about myself was gone. The relationships with the adults indicated I was one person, but this new information meant I was someone else – meant they were someone else. But, who *was I*? I'd spent time between two houses, but suddenly I didn't feel at home anywhere. In the space between the revelation and the relationship, Satan took full advantage. Like any skilled trapper, waiting and watching for the exact time your prey is most susceptible to ambush requires patience and tenacity, and this was prime opportunity. With a cruelty in his tone that would accompany many runaway thoughts and emotions in the future, the enemy whispered his counterfeit truth over me: "You don't belong anywhere or to anyone. You're all alone in the world and no one wants you, no one loves you. *You don't even know your name.*" Those words rang like an accusatory alarm in my ear and even louder in my heart. It would be many years before I came to realize that was the precise moment my spiritual identity was taken by the one Scripture calls "thief", "accuser" and "father of lies".

What was the moment your identity was taken? Your story is not identical to mine, but you have one: you were a wife and one piece of paper said you weren't. You were a mother and one lab result said you weren't. You were a best friend and one social media post said you weren't. You were an innocent and one decision said you weren't. You were a diligent employee and one Human Resources department said you weren't. You were a ministry leader and one church said you weren't. You were vital, vibrant, vivacious, and then one relationship, one outcome, one compromise said you weren't. In one breath, like me, you went from safe and secure to damaged and discarded and you *believed* it.

*In one breath you went from safe
and secure to damaged and
discarded and you believed it.*

When you don't know your name, you frantically scramble about to pick up whatever scraps someone will hand you, desperate for nourishment for your haggard, hungry heart because you just need to be known. If we have no name, then we must be nobody, so we listen to what society and media and well-meaning friends and family call us, unaware the accuser is the one craftily setting the bait to lead us farther from the truth. Before we know it, "Single" sounds an awful lot like "Insignificant", "Unemployed" can become "Unimportant" and "Childless" marks us as "Hopeless". For me, in that split second, "Orphaned" turned into "Alone", "Unwanted" and "Abandoned". This would become my reality, my identity, for decades while I searched for my new name.

I'd like to adamantly say *this was not truth*! I was none of those things and neither are you. But that's the thing about an accuser, thief and liar: he looks for opportunities to distort, deceive and devalue. "Be clearheaded. Keep alert. Your accuser, the devil, is on the prowl like a roaring lion, seeking someone to devour" (1 Peter 5:8 CEB). Several versions of Scripture use "adversary" in this passage. Satan is the enemy of any and all who belong to Jesus, and he takes great delight in hurting Him by attacking us. You see, God takes it *very* personally: "he who touches you, touches the apple of His eye" (Zechariah 2:8b). If Christ is your Savior, God is your Father, and you are sealed with the Holy Spirit (Ephesians 1:13). Nothing can snatch you from His hand, but the enemy can certainly snatch us from reality.

I read a story of a sailor from long ago who had been in prison for some time and then released. With some money in his pocket, he went to the docks and found a man with several birds for sale all in cages. The newly-freed sailor walked up to the merchant and said, "How much for all the birds you have?" After securing the sale, the man opened every door of every cage and allowed every bird to fly away. The merchant called out, "Why on earth did you buy all my birds just to let them go?" The sailor replied, "Once you've been in prison like I have, you make sure to set everything free you can get your hands on."

When you've been a captive as I have, you make it your mission to proclaim freedom to others imprisoned. It is my prayer that through this book, you will recognize whatever lies the enemy has used to entrap you. And that you will see yourself as God sees you: Holy. Royal. Chosen. *His*. "You are a chosen people. You are royal priests, a holy nation, God's very own possession. As a result, you can show others the goodness of God, for he called you out of the darkness into his wonderful light. *Once you had no identity as a people; now you are God's people....*"
(1 Peter 2:9-10 NLT)

I followed the scraps offered, unaware they were leading me into a trap that would hold me captive for many years to come. Perhaps you know what I mean – the false identity whispered in your ear begins to mold and shape your every motive, conclusion and decision. Before you can even realize or comprehend the snare you've walked in, you mistakenly start to feel at home. Like a tiny bird, so desperate for a safe place to belong, you believe the big, beautiful surroundings to be security.

And the door to the cage closes before you even see the bread crumbs leading to freedom.

Chapter Two: This is for the Birds

*"They are a people who have lost their **identity**..."*
Isaiah 23:13 TPT

Identity theft is considered the deliberate use of someone else's identity to the other person's disadvantage or loss, while mistaken identity's definition indicates it's when someone wrongly believes that one person is another person. I would like to offer my own definition of *spiritual* identity theft as a combination of the two:

The deliberate use of someone else's identity such that the person wrongly believes to their disadvantage they are another person, thereby suffering great loss.

Because I was only seven when my spiritual identity was taken, my title would be, "Miss" Taken Identity. Yours could be, "Ms.", "Mrs.", or "Mr.", with the only distinction being the title, circumstance, and stage of life. The Thief is not a respecter of age, marital status, or station. He just, *takes.*

There is much written on identity theft in the financial world with stories that are heartbreaking: unsuspecting people having their life savings swindled and their bank accounts dwindled. There are also tragic accounts of mistaken identity in news reports and books. Spiritual identity theft, however, is not as publicized or realized to be as rampant, although its victims are most assuredly unsuspecting and the accounts both tragic and devastating. I believe this is because Satan wants it quiet. If he's exposed, his tactics will be, too, and that just won't do when you're running the spiritual identity theft game. Or baiting a trap.

Mary Magdalene is a great scriptural example of mistaken identity. She has the dubious distinction of being labeled a prostitute, yet the Bible never tells us anything to support this. The details surrounding her life and reputation have widely been supposition, misinformation and assumption. This is what we know of her:

"Soon afterward Jesus began a tour of the nearby towns and villages, preaching and announcing the Good News about the Kingdom of God. He took his twelve disciples with him, along with some women who had been cured of evil spirits and diseases. Among them were Mary Magdalene, from whom he had cast out seven demons. Joanna, the wife of Chuza, Herod's business manager; Susanna; and many others who **were contributing from their own resources to support Jesus and his disciples.**" *Luke 8:1-3 NLT (emphasis mine)*

Scripture tells us Mary left her home and sacrificially gave to provide for Jesus' ministry, so we learn she was generous. Matthew's gospel tells us Mary accompanied Jesus from Galilee to care for Him, giving evidence of her devotion. Other passages reveal she stayed beside the cross, illustrating her loyalty. And that she, with two other women purchased spices in which to make our Savior's broken body burial-ready, demonstrating her courage and faithfulness to the very end. Mary left her old life before Jesus behind to serve Him and the other followers, proving her unwavering commitment.

I realize, sweet friend, you could be a generous woman who left her home and sacrificially gave to her husband. Or a devoted man who stood by a broken woman after others had ravaged her heart by running away. Or a loyal daughter, faithful friend or courageous mother standing vigil over the death bed of someone taken from you much too soon, leaving you to ensure their last needs were met after their final breath. Or, you're the one who left your old life behind with unwavering commitment to serve Jesus and serve His people – or you love someone that did.

And maybe that husband left you after you'd left everything for him. And maybe that woman's heart was so damaged by others before you, it was beyond her capability to let you in. And maybe the loneliness after the death of that one you loved has left you feeling so lost, disconnected, or bitter, you think your loyalty was ludicrous, your courage counterproductive, and your faithfulness a failure. And maybe, just maybe, the reality of serving Jesus and His people requires more than you think you can give, leaving you feeling like a failure and a fraud. And you wonder, *is it worth it?*

These are the times we hear words whispered over us in our exhaustion, emptiness, disillusionment and despair – the times we swallow the words until they become so much a part of us, we lose ourselves in them. These are the assumptions, the suppositions and the misinformation. These are the reputation-makers and the image-casters. These words are the things that can so overtake us with confusion and exaggeration, before we even realize what has transpired, we actually assume the false identity.

In a cage of captivity that subtly steals pieces of our innermost thoughts and feelings a little more each day, we begin to settle into the familiarity of it all.

In a cage of captivity that subtly steals pieces of our innermost thoughts and feelings a little more each day, we begin to settle into the familiarity of it all.

Psalm 124 reads like a laundry list of the perils of what could happen without the Lord being on our side. Descriptions of waters that rage and floods that engulf and torrents that sweep over are coupled with being physically attacked and swallowed alive. The attacker, with his burning anger, is depicted with teeth that can tear apart the unsuspecting bird that has been ensnared. These are vivid, painful, frightening images that are far too recognizable and much too personal:

If the LORD had not been on our side

when people attacked us

they would have swallowed us alive

when their anger flared against us;

the flood would have engulfed us,

the torrent would have swept over us,

the raging waters

would have swept us away.

Praise be to the LORD,

who has not let us be torn by their teeth

We have escaped like a bird

from the fowler's snare…

I believe if Mary Magdalene were a bird, she would be a

turtledove. Known to be quiet, devoted and faithful, turtledoves prefer the familial aspect of groups to the solidarity of isolation. These calm and peaceful birds have no peripheral vision, so their eyes only see what's right in front of them. Such tunnel vision can be their detriment if their gaze is not averted toward any danger lurking, making them particularly vulnerable to the fowler.

Perhaps this is the most familiar description of Mary of Magdala:

"After Jesus rose from the dead early on Sunday morning, *the first person who saw him was Mary Magdalene, **the woman from whom he had cast out seven demons**.*" Mark 16:9 *(emphasis mine)*

The fact that Mary Magdalene was possessed by seven demons reminds me how all-consuming spiritual warfare can be. Though one who has accepted Christ cannot be possessed, count on this – we *will* be oppressed. When Satan sets his sights on us, his method is to entirely destroy – hopes and dreams and marriages and families and ministries and life. He wants us utterly overtaken. With the totality and completion of seven, he is systematically thorough.

Satan's quest is to deliberately inflict great harm, and this fowler knows if our eyes can be averted off Christ's, we are easy prey. Notice that even after Mary was set free of her demonic inhabitants, she was still remembered for them. They were synonymously linked to her, the same way Satan intends for our past to be entangled with our present like shackles of shame. Or like a trusting turtledove caught in a snare.

Mary Magdalene lived chained to seven demons. I have lived chained to my own. My personal account of Psalm 124 could read I was, "engulfed in a flood of fear" or "swallowed alive by pride" or "swept away by comparison." These oppressions followed me into the recesses of my mind and the deepest places of my heart until I became them.

If Scripture revealed your shame-shackles, what would they be? Bitterness, abuse, unforgiveness, addiction, unbelief? Seven beautiful birds – the mockingbird, sparrow, goose, magpie, raven, peacock and swallow, will illustrate for us how we can easily be taken captive by seven different identity thieves. Together we'll learn how the enemy uses words, fear, malice, comparison, depression, pride and apathy to tear us apart from the inside out until we feel as imprisoned as our feathered counterparts.

But, take heart, Little Bird – the Lord is on your side. And we'll soon discover the lengths He will go to rescue us.

Take heart, Little Bird.
The Lord is on your side.

He upholds the cause of the oppressed and gives food to the hungry. The LORD sets prisoners free. (Psalm 146:7)

Chapter Three: If that Mockingbird Won't Sing
THIEF #1 – WORDS

*"We have been as usual asking the wrong question.
It does not matter a hoot what the mockingbird is singing.
The real and proper question is: Why is it beautiful?"*
Bertrand Russell

Legend has it that famous novelist Ernest Hemingway was in a diner with some writer friends having lunch one day and made a wager. The story goes that the author bet his friends ten dollars each he could construct an entire tale using merely six words. Hemingway collected his winnings after passing around the table what he'd jotted down on a napkin: "For sale: baby shoes, never worn."

Whether fact or fiction matters not. What we glean from

this account is that there is power in the spoken word.

I read once somewhere that a mockingbird is the most talented at disguising their songs. Because of this, you may never know which tune is truly theirs. That, if you think you hear several different birds outside your window on any given day, take a look. It really may be one lone mockingbird singing. They take what someone else voiced over them and, somehow along the way it became their soundtrack.

The night in the living room when my spiritual identity was taken, these words spoken over me became my background music, playing on repeat throughout my young life:

> *Who will I belong to now?*
> *I'm all alone in this world.*
> *Will I ever feel safe again?*

Words pierce and poke and prod until we bleed and bruise and break. They destroy identity faster than you can say, "broken." Words can mutilate a marriage, ruin a reputation, smother self-esteem, and choke the very life of a child. Or steal the song of a mockingbird. And it was words that began the breaking in the beginning.

---

*Words began the breaking
in the beginning.*

Now the serpent was more crafty than any of the wild animals the LORD God had made. He said to the woman, "Did God really say, 'You must not eat from any tree in the garden'?" (Genesis 3:1)

Words beckon the breaking within the woman. Eve, upon hearing Satan's winding of words spoken over her starts to believe with one leading question that perhaps there is more, perhaps she needs more, perhaps she's not enough. Perhaps God is not enough. Something breaks that day – in Eve, in all of us. With the twisting of the tale, the Crafty One fractures the confidence the Created One has in her Creator.

The woman said to the serpent, "We may eat fruit from the trees in the garden, but God did say, 'You must not eat fruit from the tree that is in the middle of the garden, and you must not touch it, or you will die.'" "You will not certainly die," the serpent said to the woman. "For God knows that when you eat from it your eyes will be opened, and you will be like God, knowing good and evil." When the woman saw that the fruit of the tree was good for food and pleasing to the eye, and also desirable for gaining wisdom, she took some and ate it..." (Genesis 3:2-6)

Standing by the tree, as the words fell from her lips, the fruit fell to the ground, and with it, our innocence. And somewhere, above in a tree that day, the mockingbird lost her own beautiful song.

That's the day we did, too. And Beautiful became Broken.

Divorce, death, dejection, the dismantling of sobriety or the dismembering of dreams – the heartache that stems from any of those things can become the anthem of a family. The roots of generational bondage run deep and reach far, and they speak over us we have to stay splintered, to live in the less-than. The trauma that reaches through generations of breaking began in Genesis 4 when Eve's son Cain killed his brother Abel. His body lay broken, his blood spilling on the ground. Blood that cried out to God to make right this broken beginning in the family tree.

Maybe the constraints of generational sin have held you captive. You cry out to God to make right the bondage spoken from within your family tree. Words of death that hang over your life, even now. Words that have spoken you'll never be free from what broke you, the curse that killed your confidence and spoke your sentence – you are destined to repeat what's always been, from the beginning. And your song is one of generations before you – of mistakes and misery and harm and hurt and grief and guilt. And the pieces lay shattered and scattered and you just want someone to put you back together. You just want to be whole.

The female mockingbird does not sing as often as the male, and her melody is much quieter. I wonder what's been spoken over you, Sweetest One. Words spoken by a physician in a hospital room. A friend in a dorm room. A family member in a living room. Someone you love who said they loved you in a bedroom. Something you spoke over yourself over and over again because that's now your theme song. If you could reduce the events in your life to a six-word narrative, could these be the words spoken to scarce and still your song?

Big empty house, big empty heart.
My arms ache for a child.
Somewhere, sometime, someone will want me.
Results show the cancer has returned.
I just want a real friend.
I can never outrun my past.
I just don't love you anymore.
I really am broken beyond repair.

It's said that mockingbirds can survive as long as twenty years in captivity. The length of everyone's prison stay by words spoken over us varies, but the aftermath of the breaking of our hearts, our minds and our spirits is the same. We remain imprisoned, listening to the words because we don't know which voice is our own. The longer we're ensnared, the more difficult discerning truth from torment becomes so we adopt the deceptive song of the Crafty One and sing right along. And Broken becomes our identity.

The Japanese believe you don't throw away damaged things. Through a method called Kintsugi, meaning "golden repair", they will take ceramics or pottery or glassware that have been smashed, even in a thousand pieces, and fill in those cracks and crevices and specks and spaces with gold. It takes what was scattered and shattered and makes it whole. The piece that was in pieces is now precious, because the gold speaks a better word than worthless. This method of restoration makes the broken even more beautiful.

When my first granddaughter was born, I had the great privilege of spending time with her on the first night home. There, in her nursery, I rocked and prayed over Adeline. I asked Holy Spirit to hover and sing over her every night in that little bed, a song known only to her. His voice, all her days, singing over Adeline *their* song. My prayer from that very first night, from her beginning, was that she would readily recognize His voice, His song, above all others competing when He called her to Himself one day.

He has a song over you, too, Sweet Mockingbird. His

lyrics are not about leaving, His refrain not about ridicule, His music not about mourning. He sees each piece of you, the ones you think no one sees, the ragged and jagged pieces and parts of your broken and battered heart and He cradles them in His mighty, gentle, healing hands. The places you think no one would assign any value, or ever come near. But He does. He's not afraid of your broken, because He doesn't throw away damaged things. He picks them up and puts them back together until you're one original song again.

He has a song over you, too,
Sweet Mockingbird.

What I did not know that night in the living room, what Eve did not know that day beside the tree, what you may not know today inside yourself is, there has always been One singing a song over us. It's a melody of love, written just for us. Just for *you*. Your own original score. With your pain, your past, your desires and your dreams in mind. It's a quiet ballad of forgiveness, of redemption, of wholeness, of worth. Of enough. Oh, if we would only lean into our not-enough, we would see that Jesus is, that we are, because of Him, very much enough. His strength, His wisdom, His purity, His love, His trust, His faithfulness, His beauty. It's all enough. We are, because *He is*.

If you listen, you will hear the quiet singing of Father over you:

> *I have always believed in you.*
> *Your past is safe with Me.*
> *I am enough – you are enough.*
> *You are not what you've done.*
> *No matter who leaves, I stay.*
> *My heart will always choose yours.*
> *I want all your broken pieces.*
> *Mine is a song of freedom.*

Standing beside a tree we lost our song. Hanging upon a tree was Freedom's Song. The Creator came to break down barriers and crack open cages. To crush generational curses. To take the shattered and scattered and make them whole. The Thief tormented. Jesus triumphed. When

Satan's words stole our song, Jesus' Blood spoke our salvation. At a beautiful tree we believed we're not enough and at a Beautiful Tree we know we're not. But, He is. His Blood that filled in the cracks and crevices and specks and spaces of pieces of our past always speaks a better word. His method of restoration is that His blood will tell you what you're worth – priceless.

And with that, Broken becomes Beautiful.

...And by Jesus only speaking a word of healing over them, they were totally set free from their torment..." *(Matthew 8:16 TPT)*

Chapter Four: Take These Broken Wings
THIEF #2 – FEAR

"Are not two sparrows sold for only a penny?
But not one of them falls to the ground
without your Father knowing it."
Matthew 10:29

In the fourth verse of Second Samuel chapter four we read about Mephibosheth, grandson of King Saul of Israel. When he was a child, his father and grandfather died in battle. The death of the nation's leaders meant David would now take the throne. Since it was customary at the time for the new ruler to eliminate any of the remaining members of the royal family, the frightened caretaker picked up the little boy and fled and, in her haste to escape, dropped him to the floor. Scripture tells us the aftermath from this one event changed Mephibosheth's life forever – it left him unable to walk. Fear of what the nurse thought she knew of the one taking the throne changed everything.

Because Mephibosheth was vulnerable, he was easily affected by the actions of another with a mindset of mistrust. He believed he had no rightful place with the one on the throne, so he never even approached him. He remained in hiding, forgetting who he was. Whether it was intentional or not, the one in control of the situation taught him to fear the king of Israel, and he took what the influencer demonstrated and made the fright his own.

Satan influences us, too – and we take what he gives. He desires to control situations by deliberately teaching us to fear the King of Kings, keeping us in the shadows, hidden from the truth. We crawl through life crippled, afraid to approach God with our fear. *We never even try.* Mephibosheth lived his life handicapped by these things, but he just needed one person unafraid to tell him fear was not his identity, that his legacy was not that of ruin.

That's what fear does – it ruins. Fear of intimacy, fear of abandonment, fear of failure, fear of imperfection and fear of loss. We can't follow our dreams, because we're afraid to try – and fail – again. We won't pursue honest relationships with people who genuinely care about us because we may get hurt – again. We don't ask for help from friends or family because we're scared of seeming anything less than perfect – so we keep our truest selves to ourselves and live in the ruins of the fall, and the remains of the fear. And we keep quiet, keep to ourselves and keep away from the One on The Throne.

When Mephibosheth fell to the ground, so did his freedom, like a sparrow with a broken wing. It is said after this event, a bird will never be able to fly like they did before. Is this assumption based on the bird being afraid of getting hurt again? Of thinking this is all the world will be? Of remembering what life was like before fear took away freedom?

These certainly can be our struggles – thinking we are only as brave as our broken wing allows.

We think we'll never be more than the one dropped on the floor.

Fear will break our wings like nothing else. But there is something deep within that wants to – has to – believe that what broke our wing didn't break us. That we will fly again, maybe even higher than before. Perhaps that's why according to folklore, the sparrow is one symbol of freedom. Interesting, considering it's something these small, unassuming birds care little about. They can be found constantly chirping in large groups called flocks. Sparrows choose to gather where humans do, yet people place little value on their tiny lives. They are not boisterous, loud or anything but gentle. They are just happy to fade into the background, nesting near the very ones that consider them bothersome, trivial and in the way. My heart is tender toward these fragile birds, considered nuisances by the very ones they gravitate toward.

There is something deep within that wants to – has to – believe that what broke our wing didn't break us.

My heart is also so tender toward you, Little Sparrow – battling fear that makes you feel the same way. Believing what's bothering you to be bothersome to others, you won't speak up for yourself and ask for help. You consider what weighs you down to weigh on people's nerves, so you won't talk to those closest to you. You feel your trials to be trivial, so you won't take them seriously. You won't even pray about them anymore, because you "should be better than this." Satan makes sure the fear that broke your wing breaks your worth.

Fear thrives on three things: seclusion, silence and self-esteem. So we are content to quietly fade into the background existing near people but not engaging, just like the sparrow.

Fear isolates - Satan convinces us "good" Christians don't get scared. Believers never struggle with belief. The godly never have godless ideas. Faithful can't be faithless. And Warriors are just not worriers. Are you afraid to talk about what scares you – because if you say it out loud, it may come true? It can feel as if your own breath can bring your fears to life. Thoughts of death and disease and divorce. Thoughts of harm and hurt and heartache. Thoughts of either of history repeating itself or of having no future at all. And sometimes of both. Satan wants us quiet, so truth won't be spoken over the lies fear always spews. If you remove the oxygen from a room, life goes. If you remove lies, fear goes. So the one with the influence muzzles your mouth then throws you in a pit – and you're terrified to move. You're afraid to ask for help, yet afraid to be alone, so you keep quiet and keep it to yourself. Pushing to get out, you don't realize you're pushing people further away. And from the depths, you long for someone to come near. After a while, you believe no one ever will. So, the pit becomes your protection, and you stay put.

Fear instigates - Fear causes us to forget. We forget who we are and more importantly, *Whose.* All Mephibosheth had to do was remember – he was the grandson of the king. Satan loves for children of The King to forget they are protected, set apart and lacking nothing. He will use fear as a sinister stranglehold on us, choking the very identity Jesus literally died to supply. Though royal, Mephibosheth lived in fear and faded into the aftermath of the fall. A fall will do that. One bad relationship makes you afraid of commitment. One lapse in judgment makes you afraid of intimacy. One trust in the wrong person makes you afraid of failure. Satan whispers that you're damaged goods, or no good at all. That you have no right because you're not whole. This is where we stay trapped – in the belief that where we fell is where we must stay, hidden in obscurity, spiritually crippled. We see ourselves as unworthy of The King's attention. Or even worse, that He has some agenda for us because of our frailties. So in fear we remain. And The Instigator is all too happy to help.

Fear imitates - A counterfeit and a coward, fear makes us think we're playing it safe by not chasing dreams, taking chances, or walking out the calling God has placed on our lives. If fear can convince us we are safe by sitting still, we're limping through life, just like Mephibosheth. It is a hostage-taker, keeping us from intimacy and authenticity and the things that we long for, pray for, beg for. To have a family. To be loved. To use our gifts. To be useful again. It ruins friendships and confidence and relationships and chances. We will never step out, speak up or stand for anything, because we're afraid to even try. To squash a dream, a vision or a passion is heinous. And just like a terrorist hijacking hope, Satan knows we're a threat to him if we believe God, so he convinces us to sit still, be silent and never pursue the goodness of grace. Fear falsifies our future, convincing us we will never be more than a sparrow with a broken wing.

Jesus has quite another viewpoint about the sparrows, just as He does about you and me.

"Don't be afraid of those who threaten you. Don't be afraid of those who want to kill your body; they cannot touch your soul. Fear only God, who can destroy both soul and body in hell. What is the price of two sparrows – one copper coin? But not a single sparrow can fall to the ground without your Father knowing it. And the very hairs on your head are all numbered So don't be afraid; you are more valuable to God than a whole flock of sparrows." *(Matthew 10:26a, 28-30 NLT)*

Jesus tells us not to fear the things of this world – He says to "fear" only God. This means to respect and revere Him, never to be afraid of Him. To acknowledge Him as the One in absolute control. To remember nothing happens that doesn't pass through His mighty hand. The One on The Throne defeated death and hell – and fear. He conquered and took it back from the enemy when He rose from the grave on the third day. The One with *all* authority lets us know He is not afraid of fear, and that fear is *not* our identity.

---

*The One with <u>all</u> authority lets us
know He is not afraid of fear, and
that fear is **not** our identity.*

Jesus says sparrows are worth much to God and He knows where and when they fall. If they break their wing, He is right there to pick them up and mend it. He doesn't miss a thing in the life of these precious birds, and even if everyone else counts them out, He never will. He says the same about you, Sweet Sparrow.

If Jesus knows all about the sparrow, how much more does He know about you? If He values the ones society devalues, how much more are *you* worth?

What Mephibosheth obviously did not know was that he had a friend on the throne. There was a covenant made before his time, one of provision and protection. Of rescue and restoration. One that, had he known about, he'd never have lived in isolation and fear, forgetting who he was, afraid to approach the throne (1 Samuel 20:14-17, 42). The one on the throne had a plan for him, but Mephibosheth hobbled through life in fear. The king had no intention to harm. He never did. The kind, generous king wanted to restore what was rightfully his, as a child of royalty.

Years later, true to His promise, David sent for Mephibosheth, and when the king saw him, he said:

*"I will **restore** to you all the land that belonged to your grandfather Saul, and you will always eat at my table." So Mephibosheth ate at David's table like one of the king's sons. (2 Samuel 9:7b,11b)*

We bring nothing. He brings everything. To the lame and the limping, to the reluctant and the ruined, The One on The Throne restores. This word in the original Hebrew means, "being freed of any circumstance of degradation or destruction." One act of fear imprisoned Mephibosheth, and one act of faithfulness set him free. What fear sets out to ruin, love always restores.

What fear sets out to ruin,
love always restores.

Jesus spoke tenderly about the sparrows not having to fear as a model for our lives. We only have to look at their example to see what to do when fear threatens our freedom:

Remember you are Royal – The one on the throne *chose* to bestow honor, in spite of the fact that one with the broken wing could offer nothing in return. This is the essence of grace. We did nothing to deserve the gracious hand of Christ reaching for us, but He did. He extends His hand to us right where we fell, and says, "Do you want to be healed?" (John 5:1-9). He wants to make us whole and healthy and His. We brought nothing to this royal life, and there's nothing we can do to have it taken. A royal is birthed or married into regality – they are born or chosen. We are reborn *and* chosen. Speak this confidently over yourself when your fears threaten to make you forget – *"I. Am. Royal."* The sparrows know who they belong to, and never have a worry. They live like they're free. Remember you are child of The One on The Throne, and that gives you access to every good thing from you Father's kind and generous heart. Know this, and live free.

Find your flock – Even the smallest of sparrows are left alone by predators when enclosed by their flock. Look at your life and see who surrounds you. Do those closest encourage your walk with Jesus? Do they pray with and for you? Will they speak peace over your fearful heart and stay until truth triumphs? If you don't have a flock of your own, ask Father. Your heart is so precious to Him, and He knows exactly who you need. Let Him choose for you. I have a flock who gather around a table with me to meet and study The Word week after week. They hold me accountable. I have a flock of four that just make me want to run hard after Jesus. They are my safe place. I have a flock of three that fervently pray for and with me. They keep me fortified. And I have a flock of two that inspire me to go deeper, pressing in with all I have to the very presence of God. They make me brave. They are all gifts, handpicked by God Himself and are absolutely essential.

We don't have to have the loudest voice to be heard, but

we do have to say something. Speak up when you're afraid. Trust that the One that knows each number of hairs on your sweet head, knows just the flock your sweet heart needs. When fear comes, let's do as the sparrow and lean into our flock. The number has nothing to do with it – all you need is just one person not afraid of fear.

Take it to The Throne – Jeremiah chapter thirty-one tells us there was a covenant made before our time, one of provision and protection˙ Of rescue and restoration. One, that, if we will only remember, we'll never live in isolation and fear, forgetting who we are, afraid to approach The One on the Throne. Because of Jesus, we can boldly approach The Throne of Grace, without fear (Hebrews 4:16). We are forgiven, our sins are forgotten, and we, like the sparrows, know and are known by Him. You have a Father who will come to you, right in the fear, and never leave. You are not a nuisance, or a bother to Him. Just call on Him. He is right there – in the silence, in the shadows, in the seclusion.

One of my favorite passages is Lamentations 3:55-57, and I repeat it often when afraid:

"I called on your name, LORD, from the depths of the pit. You heard my plea: "Do not close your ears to my cry for relief." You came near when I called you, and you said, "Do not fear."

Jesus knows all about us, broken wing and all, and chooses us anyway.

Jesus knows all about us, broken wing and all, and chooses us anyway. We always have a place beside Him at His table. He comes to us right where we fell and restores us, every time. God has always come for us – walking in the cool of the evening in The Garden, passing through a smoking firepot with a promise, in the white-hot flames of a burning bush, a glory-filled cloud by day and all-consuming fire by night. From a pit to a palace, from the magnificence of heaven to the minuteness of a manger. He will always remember His promise, always grant grace, and always, always rescue the fearful and the fallen. In Christ, we are never again the one on the floor. We were made to soar.

So take your broken wing and fly high, Little Sparrow. Your legacy is that of royalty, never again of ruin.

Chapter Five: Birds of a Feather Flock Together
THIEF #3 – MALICE

"The snow goose need not bathe to make itself white.
Neither need you do anything but be yourself."
Lao Tzu

Did you know that a baby goose doesn't know it's a goose? Immediately after they hatch, these birds will imprint – gain their sense of species identification – on whatever living creature larger than itself that it sees. If the hatchling views a human first, they will think themselves human. It is imperative for their identity that they imprint with other geese, or they will never know who they were created to be. These innocent goslings can't yet recognize a predator – they just want to survive. The one larger-than-life makes their mark on the goose as long as it lives.

This resonates in the deepest places of my heart. Because I longed to belong, I quickly would take on the qualities of whoever larger-than-life entered my life – predator or not. Because I was desperate for a name, the imprint covered my very being like a garment. Or like a goose down coat. Does this speak into your heart as well? Have you searched for your identity in people or places or things you were never meant to? When we do this, we take on the qualities of those things. Our actions and words and thoughts are of those of who made their mark on us.

The goose is a fascinating and often misunderstood creature. Known to be vicious, they communicate with loud, honking noises to deter a predator, rival or anyone that makes them feel threatened. Their instinct to protect themselves and those they care for is strong and unmistakable, and they're known to attack without hesitation. Constantly on alert, they have excellent vision and pay close attention to body language of both people and animals – they're always sizing someone up.

May I be transparent with you? I have at times, made a goose of myself. I have been vicious. I've "honked" a few times – loudly, I might add – when I felt threatened. Sadly, I've been known to attack without hesitation in an effort to protect either myself or those I care about. And not in the noble, "righteous anger" kind of way, either. In the sizing-up-a-person-before-I-have-all-the-facts-imagination-running-loose-as-a-goose kind of way. *Birds of a feather flock together*, you might say.

Geese are covered in their down feathers at birth. The down of birds is a layer of very soft, fine feathers underneath the tougher exterior ones. I believe feelings such as jealousy, anger, bitterness, envy and malice are our exterior feathers covering up the tender down of our hearts. They're covering our pain but also our shame. Reactions like these are all too familiar to someone who's been imprinted by someone or something larger than life. I think we're loud to cover up silent insecurity. I think we attack first to avoid the hurt of abandonment. I think we study and survey body language so long that we think we're experts on whether someone is genuine or not. And we never let them get close enough to see beyond the façade of our own feelings of inadequacy. We put up our own tough exterior and work hard to protect our downy interior.

Nothing will leave a mark on a heart like shame. *Nothing.*

---

*Nothing will leave a mark on a heart
like shame. **Nothing***.

There are scars on mine from foolish things I've done in an effort to find love. To find friendship. To find healing. Oh, Sweetest One, can you relate? The pain from regret can render a person totally resentful. The embarrassment from misplaced trust can make you absolutely miserable. The humiliation from being fooled can cause great fury. We envy what others have because *we* feel we don't have enough. We're jealous because we feel *we're* not enough. We're angry because we feel *someone else* is not enough. And we're bitter because nothing is *ever* enough. We want what we don't have and we have what we don't want. And the impact from Satan, the predator of man leaves an imprint on our lives until we wear his trademark – shame.

I want to take a moment and speak to that one person reading this who was impacted by someone larger-than-life that turned out to be a traitor of your trust. Whether a friend or someone you loved, they left the mark of shame that you carry to this day. You let yourself be vulnerable – you shed your tough exterior feathers and completely opened your tender downy heart to them – only to be wounded. And the rejection and pain of the betrayal has left you feeling like you'll never be able to open yourself up again. You feel like a fool for following them, for confiding in them, for believing them. Please hear me – *you do not need to feel ashamed.* You do not need to put up walls around your precious heart. You do not need to push people away in an attempt to hurt them before they hurt you. You do not need to be anyone but who God made you to be. Like the sweet baby goose, we won't always recognize a predator – we just want to survive. We just want to belong. We just want to be loved. We just want be part of something and someone larger than life. You know what? God intentionally created that desire to love and be loved deep within us, for our broken hearts to resemble His beautiful one.

Hundreds of years ago, it was customary for families to purchase bolts of the same fabric to make their clothes. Everyone within the community would know right away who you belonged to by what you wore. They were easily identified because the design was the same. They were "cut from the same cloth". Or birds of the same feather, so to speak.

God created our broken hearts to resemble His beautiful one.

We were made in the image, in the likeness, of God. The Hebrew word *tselem* means "resemblance". We are a representation of His design, meant to display His attributes to the world. He imprinted us with Himself. We were intended for all to know we were cut from His cloth, a bird from His feather. To resemble Him. After Adam and Eve's encounter in Genesis three with the serpent – the representation of Satan – the representation of God remained *on* us, but the resemblance shifted *in* us. In an instant, the imprint of sin was etched on our heart and we took off the covering from the Father of Life and started wearing the clothing of the father of lies. We cloaked ourselves to conceal the shame of sin. The Identity Thief caused an identity crisis within us.

No one had to teach us to lie or be angry or selfish. To be unkind or lash out in frustration. To be easily offended and hold a grudge. These reactions come from the natural tendency we have from the impression made on our lives by Satan the Predator. They come from a wounded heart. Before Jesus, we were identified by our sin nature and wore those "clothes". Ephesians 4:18 says we were separated from the life God intended for us because our hearts were hard – like the tough exterior feathers on a goose. But, praise God, He who is larger than life has another way:

That, however, is not the way of life you learned when you heard about Christ and were taught in Him in accordance with the truth that is in Jesus. You were taught, with regard to your former way of life, to put off your old self, which is being corrupted by its deceitful desires; to be made new in the attitude of your minds; and to put on the new self, created to be like God in true righteousness and holiness." (Ephesians 4:20-24)

Jesus made a way for us to be who we were always intended to be. He took our sin and shame to the cross with Him and left them there. When we accept Him as our Savior, we are sealed – imprinted – with Holy Spirit, identifying us as a new creation. If we will shed our tough exterior feathers and allow Him into the soft downy interior of our hearts, that old garment we put on in The Garden will be gone for good! We put on His Robe of Righteousness. This doesn't mean we won't still struggle with feelings of malice, jealousy, anger, and bitterness. Because we're human, we have to daily put off those old garments and make the choice to put on our new ones. It's a conscious decision, because our attitude needs a constant change of clothing:

Clothe yourselves with the Lord Jesus Christ and forget about satisfying your sinful self. (Romans 13:14 NCV)

I can tell when I've been wearing those old clothes, just by my attitude driven by my thoughts. You see, jealousy, offense, unforgiveness, lashing out in anger – all start in the mind. Satan uses our sin nature against us by whispering his lies and we believe it. We hear about mutual friends having lunch one day. Satan tells us we were left out intentionally – and we're offended. We sit next to someone in Bible Study who just moved in her new home. Satan whispers ours isn't good enough – and we're jealous. Someone is asked to serve in a leadership role we're interested in. Satan says we deserve it, not them – and we become bitter. Our pastor's wife doesn't speak to us at church. According to Satan, she ignored us – and we're angry.

These reactions will remain our default unless we daily – as in *every day* – put them off. We must be intentional about it.

My husband, youngest daughter and son-in-law go to Nicaragua as often as they can to serve the people there. They tell me of a fascinating custom observed on New Year's Eve. They will fashion a man from their old clothes by stuffing them with straw and paper and fireworks. At midnight, they will light a match and let the old burn away to make way for the new. Old man out, new man in. This is such a great visual to me, and one I try to practice daily. I will imagine the events of the day before as clothing on a figure of straw. First thing in the morning, I will confess the flaws and frailties and failings of yesterday as I mentally light a match. I ask Holy Spirit to burn away the remains from the previous day's mistakes and give me His new clothing for this new day. I make the choice to put on Christ and depend on Holy Spirit's power to walk this out, not mine. I'm so grateful His mercies really are new each and every day!

Since God chose you to be the holy people he loves, you must clothe yourselves with tenderhearted mercy, kindness, humility, gentleness, and patience. Make allowance for each other's faults, and forgive anyone who offends you. Remember, the Lord forgave you, so you must forgive others. Above all, clothe yourselves with love, which binds us all together in perfect harmony. (Colossians 3:12-14 NLT)

One of the things I loved learning about geese is that the females will make strong familial bonds with the others in their group. When flying south for the winter, if one lags behind due to injury, fatigue or health issues, they will all rally with the one having difficulty. If one stops, they all stop. Their strength comes from one another in times of struggle. We can do this, too. If we are the one struggling with negativity toward others in our group – those we live with, do life with or worship with – let's practice loyalty. We can choose to not be offended. We can choose to believe the best about someone. We can choose to bless instead of curse. The same goes if we're on the receiving end of hurtful things from someone having difficulty. Let's choose to extend grace. Let's choose to shed our tough outer exterior and allow the love of Jesus access to our soft downy interior. After all, it could be us lagging behind next time. By this, we show the world how very much we resemble the One larger-than-this-life who gave *His* life to give us new life.

We don't have to work to be anything other than who God intended for us to be. He accepts us, tough exterior and all. If we let Him, He will shape our wounded, tender downy interior to make us more and more like His Son. Because of Jesus, everyone can know right away who we belong to – Him. We just need to show the world how very much we resemble our Father.

And, you know what? He looks absolutely beautiful on you.

"Imitate God, therefore, in everything you do, because you are his dear children." (Ephesians 5:1 NLT)

Chapter Six: A Bird in the Hand is Worth Two in The Bush

THIEF #4 – COMPARISON

"I have a Magpie mind. I like anything that glitters."
Roy Thomson

I have a confession. I don't have any social media footprint. As in – none. No Facebook, Twitter, Instagram, Snapchat or any other accounts. I'm a social media ghost, according to Urban Dictionary. Now, I wish I could tell you the reason is that I'm super-spiritual and I'm spending the time memorizing entire books of The Bible. Or working at a pet rescue. Or learning a second language. I *wish* I could tell you those things but, nope – the real reason I don't participate is because I can't. It's not good for me. I get caught up in the comparison trap before you can say "follower" and I become someone I don't want to be – quickly.

Now, don't get me wrong – I'm not saying social media is bad. Not at all. I'm saying it's bad for *me*. Holy Spirit has gently and graciously revealed particular struggles within my heart and convicted me of the person I become when I'm not attentive to a stronghold. It's just too difficult for me to see someone else's life and not compare my own. The enemy uses this against me by dangling the bait of feeling prideful one minute, "Look at the great life *we* have" – then pitiful the next – "Look at the great life *they* have." I see the shiny, sparkly, shimmering world of others and suddenly mine seems simple and stale and sedate. It's a slippery slope, this cage of comparison. And I slide right in every time.

Magpies are said to be attracted to glitter and glitz. It's rumored they like to decorate their nests with what shines and sparkles and shimmers, and will take whatever strikes their fancy – even if it belongs to someone else. This concept speaks to me as a woman. I like where I nest to seem glamorous, and I will metaphorically take it wherever I can get it – even if it belongs in someone else's nest. This is comparison in a nutshell. Looking at someone else's life beside our own and seeing neither clearly.

In Genesis 16, we read of two women, Sarai and Hagar. Sarai was the wife of Abram. Hagar was Sarai's servant. One the mistress of the house, one the maidservant – they couldn't be more different. The chapter opens with a collision of comparison between the two women:

Now Sarai, Abram's wife, had borne him no children. But she had an Egyptian slave named Hagar; so she said to Abram, "The LORD has kept me from having children. Go, sleep with my slave; perhaps I can build a family through her."Abram agreed to do what Sarai said. (Genesis 16:1-2)

In their culture, to be infertile meant you were cursed, as children were considered a blessing from God. Sarai's own words indicate she felt He had "kept from" her a child she so desperately wanted, even though God had promised Abram repeatedly He would be the father of many (Genesis 17:4). To neglect is to willfully disregard someone under your care. Sarai felt Father God intentionally withheld the blessing of children from her, that He neglected to care for her deepest desire to be named someone's mother. That He neglected to care about *her*. So, what do you do when you desperately want a name? You take it however you can get it.

Notice the irony in the fact that Sarai refers to Hagar as "my slave" – she does not speak Hagar's name, the very thing she longs for. The Neglected One has made Hagar nameless. Taken from her life in Egypt to be a servant, Hagar would never know the legitimacy of a home and family of her own. She would not have the attention or affection of anyone, ever. Her body would be used as means to an end as long as she lived, unless someone set her free. She would not be known or noticed for anything but that. So, what do you do when you desperately want to be noticed? You take it however you can get it.

Sarai looked at Hagar and saw opportunity for what she wanted most – a name. So, Hagar's body was used to achieve motherhood. But, what about for Hagar? For just a moment, did she have opportunity for what *she* wanted most? I have to wonder if she felt like I have in the past. Attention feels an awful lot like acceptance if you close your eyes and pretend it is. And, if you want it badly enough, to be noticed feels an awful lot like you're known. Like you have a name.

If this is striking a tender chord within your heart, you are not alone. Each of the scenarios are painfully familiar – the thought I was neglected by God in the desperate desire for a child. And the reality of not being known or noticed for anything except what I could give from my body as a means to an end. I wonder if anyone reading this has ever traded attention for real affection and being noticed for being truly known. Comparison is a cruel cage of contrast.

Comparison is a cruel cage of contrast.

Have you ever felt the ache of feeling neglected? If you have, it means you feel forgotten. It means you feel forsaken. Because my identity was so wrapped up in a name, I worked and worked for validation. I thought someone else's last name taken as my own would finally make me whole. So, I waited for adoption to give me authenticity. Then I looked for love to make me legitimate. And marriage and motherhood to make me feel that I mattered, because I yearned to be like everyone else.

Comparison is all about wanting what you think will make you complete.

Beautiful Magpie, have you chased after glitz and glimmer dangled before you in an effort to find your worth? Have you been searching for the brightness and brilliance of acceptance? Have you been blinded by the shimmer and sheen of images in your mind of what life should be? Have you held these images against your own existence and felt empty? Have you placed your identity in identification, looking for a name? Have you or someone else made you feel you were only known or noticed because of your body? Have you felt neglected by someone? By God?

We work so hard to gain from others what only Father can give because we're searching to fill a void in our hearts only meant for Him. We settle for what looks like love, because we think it's our last or only chance. We trade our innocence to be like everyone else when we really want to be unique. We take our bodies to endless extremes in the name of beauty when we're actually killing ourselves. Satan causes us to believe we've been neglected, so we take matters in our own hands when we don't feel we have the blessings we see in others. Or when we don't want to wait for the work He wants to do in us. When we do this, we rob ourselves of what God wants to demonstrate – the lengths He will go to show us His faithfulness. He is the promise-keeping God He's always been.

Comparison is a tried-and-true trap the evil one uses. He dangles sparkly and shiny in front of us in an effort to distract and distort. We place our value in the filtered frame of a photograph, the false facsimile of life from a television or movie screen and the flirtatious fascination from a website. If we look at our lives compared to our perception of someone else's, ours will always, always, come up short. But, it's *our* perception, not reality. What Satan does is try to convince us that we're different from those we think have everything we want. Here's the real truth – we all want the same things. It just looks different from the outside looking in.

Sarai and Hagar both wanted the same thing – to be known. Each was longing for what the other had in their nest. Satan stirred the discord between them to make their home a battlefield. To make God out to be untrustworthy. This is what he does – he has us look to the other, never ourselves, and never, ever to God. If we look to Him, we see He has a good plan. The best plan. His plan for our lives. Sarai needed a name. Hagar needed to be noticed. Both needed God. Isn't that really what comparison is at the core, after all? The desperate need to be known is because we're looking for our identity. The desire for a name is really about making one for ourselves because we believed the lie that ours is lacking.

I read that a magpie is a great example of first impressions not always being the right one. This is the nuance of comparison – what things look like are rarely what they seem. Reality shows, celebrity stories and social media posts are great examples. We don't remember that the "behind the scenes" is scripted, the photos are photoshopped and the posts are best life, not necessarily real life. Before long we can forget that my outside that you see is the same as your inside that I don't. That leader at church? He has strongholds, just like you. That girl at the gym? She struggles with self-image, just like you. The glamorous nest of your friends? They're trusting God with their finances, just like you. The glitter from the perfect marriage? That couple is asking Jesus to work in their hearts, just like you. The gleam from the children's halos? Their parents are on their knees asking for wisdom every day, just like you. Same fears, same faith. Same struggles, same Savior. What we think is perfection is actually the act of being perfec*ted* – and only Christ does that. *Isn't that a relief?*

What we think is perfection is actually the act of being perfected— and only Christ does that.

Isn't that a relief?

The magpie is one of only a few animals with the ability to recognize themselves in a mirror. Researchers placed a colored sticker on the neck of the bird and the magpie responded to their reflection. But if the sticker was black like their feathers, they didn't see themselves. The magpie could only look at themselves accurately if the one in control of the conditions offered a way. Otherwise, they lost themselves in the looking glass. In our cage of comparison, the evil one holds up a mirror with a distorted reflection, like a black sticker over our life. The one in control of the conditions of our captivity wants us to consider ourselves neglected. We can't recognize ourselves as God does because we're still looking for the shiny and sparkly image Satan uses to dangle and dazzle – and so we lose ourselves.

The thing is, comparison doesn't distinguish if the gleaming is actually glass, the twinkling is really tin foil, and the flashy is merely phony. Comparison is the lie that we have is lacking, who we are is lacking. Satan steals our identity and wants us to believe that creating a name for ourselves and being known is where we'll find happiness. The saying "a bird in the hand is worth two in the bush" means it's better to hold on to something you have than to risk losing it by trying to get something better. We work and work to take identity and legitimacy however we can get them and hang on with both hands. But, we're working to make a name Father has already given. We are trying to force a future He's already formed. And it's so much more than could ever be reflected in the limits of a looking glass. According to Jesus, it's limitless:

"A thief is only there to steal and kill and destroy. I came so they can have real and eternal life, more and better life than they ever dreamed of." (John 10:10 MSG)

Hagar has a divine encounter with the angel of the Lord

who gives her unborn child a name – Ishmael. And in turn she is given the honor of being the only one in the Old Testament to give God a name in return. El Roi – "*the God who sees me*" (Genesis 16:7-13). The name *Ishmael* in Hebrew is translated, "*Yahweh has been attentive to your humiliation.*" The one longing for attention, for affection, to be known, has been noticed by God Himself. He gives Sarai her new name Sarah, along with a promise she will have a son. And not just one child – she will be the mother of nations. Kings will come from her (Genesis 17:15-16). Jesus, the *King of Kings* would come from her. Sarah, no longer Neglected, became Mother of Many. When we leave our futures in the Hands of Father, we'll never look at someone else's nest again.

Because of Hagar, you and I understand we can have a personal encounter with the living God. We are noticed by El Roi – The God Who Sees us. We have His full attention, and His full affection. Because of Sarah, you and I have the assurance God always keeps His Word. And His way, is *always* the best way. And, because of Jesus, Isaiah 43:1 tells us we have a new name – His. The neglected one got a new name. The nameless one learned she was never neglected. And neither are you.

Sweet Magpie, what name are you trying to make for yourself? What lengths are you going to not feel neglected? You don't have to settle for the distorted view in the mirror The Thief holds up. What you have in your hands was given by God Himself, and this life, this marriage, this family, this version of you, is seen and known and noticed by Him. There is only one you, and you are beyond compare. Jesus loves you just as you are and He offers what's real, what's eternal. You don't have to look anywhere but to Him. Your Good Father sees beyond what you can and knows exactly what you need – and when.

There is only one you, and you
are beyond compare.

Trust El Roi – He is attentive to your unique situation. He sees your truest reflection. He knows your deepest desires. And He is preparing things for you even now greater than your wildest dreams.

Chapter Seven: Covered with His Feathers
THIEF #5 – DEPRESSION

"The cry of a young raven is nothing but the natural cry of a creature, but your cry, if it be sincere, is the result of a work of grace in your heart."
Charles Spurgeon

It was November 2002. We had all gathered that Sunday afternoon for a family meeting. My oldest brother would be calling from Houston to give us news from the visit with his doctor. Earlier that year, a mass on Ralph's pancreas was discovered during a routine check-up. We all prayed during those months to follow that the subsequent surgery performed to remove the tumor would also remove any sign of cancer. My family, my next-oldest brother and his family, and our mother all anxiously waited in her living room. This was *the* call.

No one spoke for a bit after Mother hung up the phone – the news was just too weighty for words. With pancreatic cancer, the prognosis is bleak as a general rule, and we were collectively and individually processing the fact that this was now our family's reality – Ralph would be gone within a year. I clearly remember the sound from the silence that fell. It was hard, and it was harsh. It was a darkness that was audible. The only thing louder to my ears than the silence was the noise of a heartbeat, but *whose*? Could I actually hear the tone of my own heart beating against the rhythm of covert tears and overt prayers? I vividly remember leaving the house and saying to my husband, "There is a heaviness to this darkness that I can literally *feel*. It's tangible."

I barely made it home before Holy Spirit spoke into my heart words so specific, I had to write them down:

A shadow's been cast on our family this week,
Looming and present, it longs to defeat.
Dark and mysterious, this shadow can be,
How can we fight what we cannot see?

That phone call was a defining moment for all of us. For my family, it marked the end of my big brother's life. For me, it marked the beginning of a season of depression – I just didn't know it yet.

Pain is universal. We all feel it. Because we live in a broken world, a broken heart is an inescapable by-product. For Christians though, sadness and sorrow, desperation and despair have all become dirty words. We sing in church that the joy of the Lord is our strength while our knees are about to buckle from the sheer exhaustion of trying to live up to the ridiculous charade of faking fine. Who in the world said we can't love Jesus and hate our situation at the same time? I can tell you who *didn't* – Jesus! Isaiah 53:3 tells us He was familiar with sorrow and that grief was an acquaintance of His, yet we treat them as strangers.

Because we live in a broken world,
a broken heart is an inescapable
by-product.

Death can bring on feelings of depression, but it's not just the death of life. It can also be the death of a marriage you fought hard to keep alive. Or the death of normalcy in your life because something catastrophic took it from you. It can be the death of a friendship that may never be restored – and honestly, may not need to be. The death of a great job without opportunity of finding another. The death of that hope-filled dream you've held on so tightly with both hands for longer than you can remember. The death of a relationship that held such promise you could actually see a future. The death of a ministry that was birthed from a calling you're certain you received. Death always marks the end of something. *Or does it?*

The raven is a bird of mystery. Because of their dark color, large size and bad reputation from literature, they are considered symbols of evil, bad omens and death. They are typically loners, preferring the company of only one or two others of their kind. In fact, if you do find a few ravens together, the group is called an "unkindness" – lending further to their unpopular status. Yet, this bird is the first mentioned by name in Scripture sent out from Noah in search for signs of life (Genesis 8:7). And, it was a raven that God used to feed the prophet Elijah in 1 Kings 17:1-7.

After announcing to the wicked King Ahab that there would be no rain, God told Elijah to go to Kerith Brook and hide. The brook was there to protect him from the drought and the Lord sent ravens to provide food. To Elijah, the birds were an especially unusual meal delivery system, because ravens were listed as one of the forbidden things to eat for Israelites (see Leviticus 11:13-15). The raven – a symbol of death – would bring life from his very own "unclean" beak. Even in the dark shadows of the threat of death, God shows His light with the promise of life. But this was more than just bread and water – Elijah wasn't aware that Father was also demonstrating His protection and provision *before* the biggest battle he would face with his enemy. And for this man of God, it was training ground for a time of depression to follow. (1 Kings 18-19)

There is a loneliness to depression like no other. Surrounded by a hundred people, you feel completely alone. You wonder how the world keeps spinning while yours is standing still, frozen in the days before. Before the diagnosis, the infidelity, the addiction, the miscarriage, the breakup, the incident, the accident. Before the loss and before the end. Before everything was torn away. Before nothing would ever feel the same again. Just – *before*. And the bearing down of the darkness can break your spirit as well as your heart. This was my reality for several weeks following Ralph's death. I could not see past the pain to the provision. I could not hear the message of healing in the midst of the hopelessness.

In chapter two, we read in Psalm 124 how David vividly describes feelings of being overwhelmed, overcome and overtaken, referring to his enemy as "the fowler'. A fowler is an individual that hunts birds. They are sneaky and subtle, looking for the weak and the wounded as easy prey. They patiently watch for the best opportunity to deceive the most vulnerable. They will transform a place that's been safe and familiar to the bird and set their trap, and the sweet bird will willingly walk right in. He takes their peace if he can't take their life. Satan is a skilled and sinister hunter himself. He waits for the moment our weak and wounded hearts make us vulnerable and then he watches us walk right into his snare. From the shadows, The Fowler taunts with words of hopelessness and heartache until the place once safe and familiar in our hearts and minds and spirits is now full of pain. He cannot physically take our lives, but he will take our peace. This is depression – feeling overwhelmed, overcome and overtaken.

There is a story from long ago that says on a cold winter night, with no heat and no food, a little boy and his widowed mother read how God sent ravens to feed Elijah. The child asked his mother if they could leave their door open that evening – he was that certain God's ravens were on their way. After a while, an official of the small town passed by and stopped in to ask about the open door. After hearing the reason, the man who had once known suffering himself said, "Please allow me to be God's raven for you." Only someone who had walked this same path could minister to them in this way.

Please allow me to be God's raven for you.

In the middle of a drought, Elijah drank daily from Kerith Brook. In the middle of a famine, Elijah was faithfully fed. And by a bird who is a scavenger – one who surrounds themselves with death. In Hebrew, Kerith means "cutting away". The root is the same that translates to the English word *eliminate.* God was cutting away any influences that could serve as Elijah's source of help other than Him. Father wanted any distractions eliminated that would prevent what Elijah needed to learn – that God was with him when the river ran and He would be with him when the river ran dry. Elijah was learning the difference in hiding *from* and hiding *in*. He was learning what it means to live in the shelter of Father's shadow while surrounded by the shadow of death. I knew that was the same shadow of darkness I felt with my family that Sunday afternoon, and as Holy Spirit continued to speak, something began to shift, and I continued to write. These were the words He inspired:

He brings to mind as I call on His Name,
That He is sovereign, remaining the same
He is in control, His motives are pure
His grace is sufficient, of that I am sure.

Ravens are among birds that will mantle. This means they spread their wings far and wide over what they've caught to keep it from predators. This is a symbol of great power. They will also overshadow their young by mantling. A symbol of protection, the raven covers what's most precious to them under their mighty mantle. A thief may attempt to take what's protected by the raven, but the mighty bird is ready to fight to the death. The imagery is magnificent – it is great power mixed with great tenderness. A predator is just no match for these powerful birds when their protective wings are outstretched. The Fowler is no match for The Father, either. No matter what Satan attempts to take from you, he is powerless against your powerful Father God. You are overshadowed with great tenderness under God's mighty mantle, because you are precious to Him.

The Fowler is no match for The Father.

As a parent, when my girls were in pain, I would take them in my arms and hide them there. Drawing them close to my heart, they knew as long as I held them, this was their shelter. I would have them place one hand on their chest to feel their heartbeat, and their other hand over my beating heart. Placing my hand over theirs, I'd say, *"You feel that? If you ever need to feel close to me, just touch your heart, because mine beats in perfect time with yours."*

We never outgrow the need to be held by someone who absorbs our sorrow. We stay in that safe and secret space of security until the pain subsides. I will hold my daughters to this day, if need be. There is such beauty to shared sorrow. It is a secret place between mother and child that is sacred. That is the essence of mantling – to completely encompass the thing that is precious to you and hide them there. They remain hidden in the shadow of the wing until the danger is gone, until the predator leaves, or until the pain passes. Nothing can touch the one covered in the shelter of the shadow, and the covered one will cling to the beating heart of their healer.

The sweetness of this truth was further echoed in the words Holy Spirit gave me as a gift for Ralph:

> *So now we cling to what we know,*
> *We hold on tightly, we won't let go.*
> *We run to The One called Faithful and True,*
> *We trust in Him – He'll see us through.*

Psalm 91 was what Father used that day to teach me He would be with me the day of Ralph's diagnosis and the day of his death. Like He did with Elijah, He was preparing me in advance for the truth I would need for my battle with the enemy – and the depression to follow. He was giving me a message as I wrote my big brother's poem – as He hid Elijah by the Kerith Brook, He was hiding me in the shadow of His wing. He was saying the darkness surrounding me that I thought was so heavy was His powerful mantle of protection. And He was telling me the beautiful beating heart I heard in the living room that day was His – the one that beats in perfect time with mine. It also beats with your broken heart today, Little Bird. Place your hand on your sweet chest. Can you feel it? Cling to the beautiful beating heart of your Healer.

Cling to the beautiful beating heart
of your Healer.

To have a person's shadow fall on you means they are *very* close. Psalm 34:18 says God is near to the brokenhearted and saves those with spirits crushed by pain. You are so precious to Jesus! He longs to gather His people up like a mama bird with her babies if we would only let Him (Luke 13:34). What I see now was that He was trying to prepare me so I would run to Him when The Fowler overwhelmed me. So I would reach for Him when the snare overcame me. So I would rest in Him when sorrow overtook me. Because we are spiritual beings, we are always either recovering from a battle or readying for one. If you are not fighting depression in this season, ask Holy Spirit to show you what He has for you right now that will be used for the future. Ask Him to bring to your mind Scripture and truth He's revealing in these days so you can turn to Jesus when you need Him in the days to come.

If you are currently in the battle of depression, please run to The Father. After Him, talk to your pastor or a godly counselor grounded in God's Word. There is no shame in your pain, no dishonor to your tears. Allow yourself to grieve, but please also allow yourself to be loved. Hide *in* Him, not *from* Him. The result is a work of grace.

The final words used to minister to me and my family then I pray bring you the same strength today:

This shadow I once thought a terrible thing,
A presence so dismal and drear,
Is nothing to fear, it means He is here,
The shadow is cast by His wing.

"Those who live in the shelter of the Most High will find rest in the shadow of the Almighty. This I declare about the LORD: He alone is my refuge, my place of safety; He is my God, and I trust him. For He will rescue you from every trap and protect you from deadly disease. He will cover you with his feathers. He will shelter you with his wings. His faithful promises are your armor and protection." *(Psalm 91:1-4 NLT)*

Chapter Eight: As Proud as a Peacock
THIEF #6 – PRIDE

"The pride of the peacock is the glory of God."
William Blake

"Who do you think you are, the Queen of Sheba?"

If this expression sounds familiar, chances are you can thank your mother or your grandmother. If you're like me, you earned this or the alternate "Miss Astor" title for being, shall we say – *too big for your britches*. I so appreciate my sweet mama for keeping my wannabe-royal feet on the ground, and when she spoke those words to me, I knew exactly what she meant. I was either full of opinions, full of drama, or full of sass. In other words, just plain full of myself. Or as proud as a peacock.

With their fabulous fanned feathers and their brilliant blue body, the peacock is one of the most recognized of birds. They are glorious creatures with very interesting ways. For instance, they will perch on a treetop, but create their nests on the earth below. They engage in game-like activities with others in their circle. They will interact with humans using big gestures, performing to get our attention. They love the sunlight. They are courageous snake-chasers, said to be the best fighter of this enemy. If you're lucky enough to see a peacock, look carefully – the color of its tail varies every time you look from a different angle.

Did you know peacocks are mentioned in the Bible? There is one inclusion of them contained in two passages of Scripture found among the listing of King Solomon's wealth (see 1Kings 10:22 and 2 Chronicles 9:21). The king had an entire fleet of ships that brought in exotic items every three years, and these beautiful birds were among the cargo. I love the fact that the mention of these majestic creatures comes immediately after the details of the Queen of Sheba's visit with the King of Jerusalem.

"When the queen of Sheba heard about the fame of Solomon and his relationship to the Lord, she came to test Solomon with hard questions. Arriving at Jerusalem with a very great caravan – with camels carrying spices, large quantities of gold, and precious stones – she came to Solomon and talked with him about all that she had on her mind." 1 Kings 10:1-2

I can't help but compare the beautiful peacock to the beautiful queen. A crown adorns the head of a royal. And also of a peacock. Both the queen and the bird have one claim to Biblical fame linked to King Solomon. And they each have an expression associating them with pride. Of the seven spiritual identity thieves, this one is the most subtle. It is easily disguised, which makes perfect sense – pride is Satan's trademark identity thief. He will manipulate us as often as he can to confuse and camouflage his true motive – using us against ourselves. For example, using "self" as a prefix can look so noble one minute: selfless, self-help, self-control. But using the same prefix can also indicate something quite the opposite: self-aware, self-destruct, self-harm. Two sides, one coin, very different meanings. Much like the double talk of The Deceiver.

The story of the Queen of Sheba's visit with King Solomon is a great parallel to the practices of the peacock – and how Satan will show us one side of ourselves, but God has something quite the opposite in mind. In fact, James 4:6 tells us that God actually opposes the proud, but to the humble He gives grace. In this passage "proud" in the Greek is *hyperephanoi,* meaning pride, arrogance or haughtiness. God will take the prefix of our pride and completely repurpose the process into grace-filled humility if we let Him. Using the behaviors of the colorful peacock, the Queen of Sheba will demonstrate for us how just one encounter with the king can change everything.

God will take the prefix of our pride and completely repurpose the process into grace-filled humility if we let Him.

Peacocks engage in games with their peers. The Queen of Sheba was curious to see if the wisest king in the land could be stumped, and traveled many miles to question

King Solomon. This was a quest to engage in a game with one who was her equal. We play games with those in our circle, too – spiritual hide and seek. We're either hiding from who we are or seeking our worth in someone else's opinion. What the enemy hides from *us* in this game that we play is the underlying pride in the approval that we seek.

Arrogance is having an exaggerated sense of one's importance or abilities. Typically, this is thought to be displayed in vanity or conceit, but to exaggerate is to portray something not as it truly is – for better *or* worse.

Precious Peacock, have you ever built yourself up before someone else could tear you down? Have you torn yourself down, only to realize you're desperate for someone to build you up? Whether we think too much or too little of ourselves, I have come to realize that at the root of pride is the feeling of insignificance. Look this word up – you'll see words like "lacking importance" "too small for consideration", "meaningless". We inflate our image because we fear we lack importance. We color our character because we think we're too small for consideration. And we magnify our material goods because we're terrified we're meaningless. Hiding me to seek from you what I think will make me significant is arrogance, and an enemy to authenticity. Much to his delight, The Deceiver watches our self-esteem ebb and flow and our self-worth wax and wane. And his cruel game with our heart continues.

Hiding me to seek from you what I think will make me significant is arrogance, and an enemy to authenticity.

Peacocks interact with humans using big gestures to perform and gain attention. When important people burst on a scene with an entourage, they are not afraid of the limelight. This is the picture in verse two of our Queen's arrival – a great caravan with grand displays of wealth. Our Greek word *Hyperephanoi* comes from two words: *hyper* meaning above, beyond or over, and *phaino* meaning to shine a light on – shining a light above yourself. This is pride – me in the spotlight. Jesus uses this word after an encounter with the Pharisees criticizing His disciples for not participating in hand-washing rituals. Pharisees were famous for showmanship and loved the limelight. But the hand washing was for ceremony, not for cleanliness, and Jesus tells them not to concern themselves with their hands, but their hearts (Mark 7:1-14). There's nothing like a heart examination to put things in perspective.

The enemy traps us with the lure of attention we get from performance so we don't have to look too closely inside. He even uses serving God to his advantage. Bible study, worship, going to church – anything we do can be twisted to look like big gestures for Jesus. We can go through the motions and check all the right boxes and feel real good about ourselves, like we're doing God a favor – and even look pretty holy to everyone else in the process. But if we never really deal with anything past surface level of the motive behind the motions, we're just washing our hands of religion without having our hearts of relationship cleansed. If we're not careful, we'll confuse the spotlight of conviction from Holy Spirit with the ceremonial limelight of the enemy and never even realize we're trying to outshine The Son.

Peacocks make their nest on the ground, but prefer the treetops. The last definition of proud is haughty – looking down on someone as if they are beneath you, much like the peacock's vantage point from the tree line. This is very enlightening to me personally. I have those in my "nest on the ground" – the closest ones I let really see me. But, if I'm honest, the majority of people view me from my treetop – I keep them at a distance. Now, as we've established, there is wisdom in trusting Jesus to choose your innermost people – your nest. But, keeping others at arm's length – or treetop distance – can be a detriment to what Christ wants to do.

Satan has convinced me for years that preventing pain and protecting privacy equals distance. Holy Spirit has gently revealed to me that what I see as guarding my heart, He sees as haughtiness. I can say all I want that I'm private and protective, but by keeping myself a safe space away, I can appear aloof or uncaring to my brothers and sisters in Christ, or to the world. Thinking myself noble and even pious by distancing myself is false modesty – the wicked stepsister of pride. Jesus let people near, even drawing them in. I never want to hinder His working in me or through me to minister to others. The Queen of Sheba was transparent with King Solomon, enough to talk with him about all she had on her mind. This was because she was responding to the Lord working through Solomon, whether she realized it or not. That never would have happened from a treetop. Keeping our nest grounded is one thing, and we should. But I also want to come down from my perch long enough to see people like Jesus does, and let them see Him, in me.

With each parallel of the peacock's behavior and the Queen of Sheba's visit so far, we see pride. This is where Satan wants the story to stop, and self to stay stuck. But, for the queen – and for us, thankfully – God has more:

"When the queen of Sheba saw all the wisdom of Solomon and the palace he had built, the food on his table, the seating of his officials, the attending servants in their robes, his cupbearers, and the burnt offerings he made at the temple of the LORD, she was overwhelmed." *(1 Kings 10:4-5)*

Don't miss this – The Queen of Sheba was overwhelmed. Depending on the version of Scripture, we read words like "breathless", "amazed", "speechless" and "in awe". It's hard to imagine a royal breathless over a palace, amazed over a meal, or speechless over servants or officials – she likely had all that in her own kingdom. Yet, this wealthy, powerful, regal woman was completely overtaken. So, what *would* inspire such awe to someone in her elevated station in life? Only someone above her. One who was greater. When the queen saw Solomon's acts of obedience and devotion to God through his offerings at the temple, she reacted the same as anyone. She was overwhelmed by the majesty of the only King worthy of worship. She encountered the presence of Jehovah in His dwelling place, and she was absolutely undone.

This is what happens when we encounter the matchless holiness of the living God – we have no choice but to *really* see ourselves. And we are left speechless. Amazed. Breathless. Awestruck. Humbled. The Queen of Sheba thought she initiated the visit with the king of Israel. What she didn't realize was The King of Kings was wooing her, just as He pursues us. He captivates a room, and He captivates our hearts. Just a whisper from His presence, and pride perishes.

---

*Just a whisper from His presence
and pride perishes.*

Just as the sweet peacock's behavior provides an illustration of pride, it also offers a picture of humility, and how to combat pride.

The color of the peacock's tail varies depending on the angle. Our passage in James tells us that we are directly opposed to God when we allow the natural tendencies of self to surface. Pride is a prison of opposition and Satan is the wicked warden. Do you ever feel like you're in constant conflict with yourself? That's the work of The Warden. He knows how inclined we are to pride, so he colors our view to his selfish vantage point – people rather than God for validation, lofty distance rather than drawing near, and religion over relationship. The enemy knows these things cause a division between us and our brothers and sisters in Christ, and a disconnection of fellowship from God. Holy Spirit works against The Warden to free us from this prison of pride. He lovingly redirects us by revealing Satan's true colors without any condemnation for our misplaced point of view. He just shows His kindness that leads to our repentance (Romans 2:4). When we look at life from the position of opposition, we are prideful. When we look through a place of grace, we are humbled.

Peacocks are courageous snake-chasers. James 4:7 says, "Submit to God, resist the devil and he will flee". In Hebrew, one word for humble is *kana*. This refers to submission. It's subduing an enemy, but also subduing your own soul first in an act of humility. The word picture is an open hand – the exact opposite of a closed fist. This is what the queen of Sheba saw in the mighty King Solomon – he submitted to God with hands open and raised in surrender to the only One worthy. The word *resist* in this passage comes from two Greek words meaning "stand" and "against". Standing firm on the authority of the powerful name of Jesus, speak it against the tricks of the enemy. The Snake cannot remain where we speak Jesus' Name! Wherever a soul is surrendered in humility, Satan has to flee. So, how do you chase a snake? Humbly submit to God and surrender your will to Him. Then stand firm on the authority of Christ and speak His Name against Satan. The

Snake will vanish, along with any hint of pride.

Peacocks love the light of the sun. I read that makeup artists agree the "daylight" setting on a lighted mirror gives the most accurate reflection of your face. The light of the sun reveals flaws and imperfections so they can be concealed – so the world won't see what we really look like. Operating in shadows and darkness, Satan masquerades as light (2 Corinthians 11:14) in order to conceal truth. Jesus *is* light (John 8:12) so we can deal with pride honestly – with Him. We don't belong to the night or the darkness, says 1 Thessalonians 5:5 – we are children of the daylight.

Pride is the lie that we are insignificant. Satan captures our self-esteem and holds our self-confidence in his snare until we feel like we're nothing. Beautiful Peacock, do you feel you have to perform to be seen? Do you think you have to become someone else to be accepted? Do you believe you have to disassociate with people and not let them know the real you? Have feelings like this made you feel so badly about yourself, your worth has fallen to the floor? You may not know this, but that's the best place to be. When we're at our lowest, Father meets us right there. Psalm 18:35 says that God stoops down to make us great. He makes us *significant*. This posture is one of great humility, but also of great affection.

My youngest granddaughter is seven months old. Whenever I see Sophie, I just can't wait to pick her up. She is absolutely irresistible to me. But what I really love is to get right down beside her when she's on the floor. I don't do this because she's beneath me – I do it because Sophie can't come to me yet. She will take her little hands and place them on my face with such sweetness. We are face to face, eye to eye, and heart to precious heart. This is affection at its purest. Sophie's learning who I am because I stoop down to let her know me. I am willing to lower myself for love. Do you know you're loved like that? With the affection of One who can't wait to pick you up when the fallout from pride sends you to the floor, you are irresistible to Him.

When Jesus left His throne in Heaven, He stooped down to let us know Him because we can't come to Him yet. He made Himself nothing for you and me, because He wanted us to see Him face to face, eye to eye, heart to precious heart. He took on the role of a servant to lower Himself for love. Humbling Himself all the way to Calvary, He died for us. He was buried and rose from the grave three days later. Today, He is seated at the right hand of the Father so we can be with Him where He is, always. This is affection at its purest. Who would stoop for you? Someone who considers you worth dying for. I'd say that makes you pretty significant, Sweet Peacock.

Who would stoop for you? Someone who considers you worth dying for.

I'd say that makes you pretty significant, Sweet Peacock.

If Holy Spirit has revealed any areas of pride, take off the concealer and face the Son. His light is warm and healing, and rather than exposing flaws, He reveals truth. His light shines in us so it can shine through us to a world living in darkness. Jesus stoops down to look us in the eye so we can see His beautiful face. This is transparency. This is relationship. This is unfailing love. This is what renders a royal humbled, and honestly, me too.

So, you can call me Queen of Sheba after all, and I will boast in that – it means I am known and loved by The King.

This is what the LORD says: "Don't let the wise boast in their wisdom, or the powerful boast in their power, or the rich boast in their riches. But those who wish to boast should boast in this alone: that they truly know me and understand that I am the LORD who demonstrates unfailing love and who brings justice and righteousness to the earth, and that I delight in these things. I, the LORD, have spoken!" (Jeremiah 9:23-24)

Chapter Nine: Winging It
THIEF #7 – APATHY

"True hope is swift, and flies with swallow's wings."
William Shakespeare

When my baby girl decided to invite her boyfriend to the house to share his first supper with our family, I was all over it. This was an important meal and I wanted to impress this important young man. I did my due diligence and tasked my daughter with finding out what her fella's most favorite food was. I was thrilled to learn it was lasagna – a dish right in my wheel house. It was the first thing my mother taught me to cook, and my mama's recipe is deliciously foolproof. Perfecting it over the years, it was often "company food," so I thought this would be effortless – except that I discovered the boyfriend's favorite version came from a popular Italian restaurant chain. Not to be outdone, I googled to find how they prepared it. I was so excited to learn there was a "copycat" recipe! I bought the exact ingredients, followed the instructions to the letter, and made the lasagna – and it was *awful*. Not exactly inedible, but far from delicious. Praise Jesus this didn't deter him, and the boyfriend eventually became my son-in-law. Evidently the love for the girl negated the taste for the food.

I learned my lesson that day, and when my oldest daughter brought her now-husband home for his first meal with the family, I stayed true to what I knew. I'd been given the very best from my mother but traded it for a flimsy imitation of someone else's idea of better. Even though the story became a long-standing joke in our family, it was rich in truth – a copycat is just a fancy counterfeit.

For something to be counterfeit, there must be the following: inferior quality, infringement on authenticity, and the intent to fool. In other words, something looks good for a while but doesn't last. Something is passed off as reputable but is actually a reproduction. Some counterfeiters will actually take pieces of the real thing and use it in the phony one, making the copy remarkably similar to the creation. Who is a target for a counterfeiter? The deceived – those unable to recognize authenticity and are easily fooled. The dissatisfied – those that are restless, always looking for something better. The distracted – those who just aren't paying attention. Or to put it another way – the apathetic.

Apathy is defined as having no enthusiasm, a lack of feeling or emotion, and demonstrating a lack of interest or energy – bored, disinterested and empty. How do we become apathetic? By auto-piloting our day-to-day, week-to-week, month-to-month routines, we're prime candidates for Satan the Counterfeiter to deceive and distract. He knows how easily we can become dissatisfied with the pace of life, and we run and run out and we give and give out, constantly on the go and going nowhere fast – like a frantic bird in flight.

The swallow is just such a bird. Always on the move, their long pointed wings and streamlined bodies enable these acrobatic songbirds to fly very fast. Continuously in motion, they will feed their babies in flight, and not stop when thirsty – they drink "on the wing". They will fly low to a body of water and dip their feathered appendage in with perfectly choreographed grace. Still in flight, they take a drink by extending their watered wing upward and letting it drip into their mouth. These beautiful birds are busy and on the go, even to the point of running the risk of starvation and exhaustion when migrating. Oh, Swift Swallow, can you relate? As a young family with two daughters, we were always going somewhere – cheerleading, tumbling, piano lessons, riding lessons. Not to mention school activities, family functions and church events. We were continuously in motion. I have often fed my babies in the flight of my vehicle and many a Diet Coke has been drunk on the wing as I speedily stuck my feathered appendage through a drive-thru window. I'm thinking many of you are experiencing this right now.

During this season of life, I wouldn't have considered myself apathetic, especially when it came to the things of God. Busy? Certainly. Involved? Absolutely. Committed? One hundred percent. Empty? Wait – *what*? I was teaching twelfth grade girls on Sunday mornings, college girls on Sunday evenings, facilitating women's Bible studies Sunday nights and co-teaching twenty-somethings with my pastor husband on Wednesday nights. If you looked at my life through the lens of good works, life was good and it worked. However, if you looked through the lens of my spirit, I was spent. I was always in The Word studying to teach, but not to learn. I was pouring everything I had into everyone but not stopping long enough to be filled myself. I was drinking on the wing tiny droplets of water when I desperately needed to drink freely from the Fountain of Life. I was the fullest empty vessel that ever was.

I was the fullest empty vessel that ever was.

"My people have done two evil things: They have abandoned me – the fountain of living water. And they have dug for themselves cracked cisterns that can hold no water at all!" (Jeremiah 2:13 NLT)

These were the words Father spoke over His children when they were chasing after copycat comfort. First, the people of Jerusalem forgot about God and turned to the idols of the neighboring countries of Assyria, Egypt and Babylon who were wealthy and self-sufficient. The people grew distracted by what looked like a life of ease and became dissatisfied with waiting for God to answer their prayers in *their* time. They were deceived by the lies that God wasn't at work in their lives, and so became an easy target for Satan the Counterfeiter. God said their idols were worthless and His children had become just like them (Jeremiah 2:5). "Worthless" in Hebrew is *habal* – empty, meaningless, something transitory that will never satisfy, full of air. It's being apathetic – filled up with emptiness.

Ecclesiastes 1:9 says there is nothing new under the sun. Satan still looks for the deceived, the dissatisfied and the distracted. We're husbands and wives creating expectations of each other based on impossible standards within our own minds. We're young adults looking for friends and relationships to fill a void in our hearts left by someone else. We're moms and dads working long hours and sacrificing our health to compete with the image of what we believe is expected of us compared to society. We're church leaders and pastors who have a sincere call to minister and serve Jesus, but concern ourselves with popular opinion rather than Holy Spirit approval.

---

*If we expect people or possessions
to fill an emotional, physical or
spiritual need, we unintentionally
make them a pseudo-savior.*

If we expect people or possessions to fill an emotional, physical or spiritual need, we unintentionally make them a pseudo-savior. To seek from them our identity, purpose and worth, not only are we placing them in an impossible position, we will inevitably begin to resent them for not being who we envisioned. And when they don't live up to the unrealistic standard we've set, the realization that sets in will be harsh – the friendship, relationship, marriage or ministry is copycat completion. We either walk away or stay, but we're filled with resentment. No matter what, we are left empty. There's a reason they will never be who and what we think we need – *they were never meant to.* No matter how wonderful that friend or family member is, they will disappoint us. Finances can be lost faster than they were gained. Eventually something or someone at church will fail our expectations.

God calls idolatry a snare (Psalm 106:36) and a bird never gets caught in a trap that has no lure (Amos 3:5). This knowledge is not meant to cause condemnation – it's meant to make you mad. We would never sit by and let someone manipulate our children or use our spouse as bait against us, yet The Counterfeiter does it all the time. We would never consider hard work and honest motives for financial security to be a temptation, but it is. And we would be appalled to think our desire to worship and serve Jesus could lead us into captivity, but it does more often than we realize.

We depend on bank accounts, church attendance, approval ratings, social media followers, credit scores, aptitude scores and scoreboards. We remember to fill our calendars and fill our lives but never see we've forgotten God. A good gauge is whether life is happy or horrible, where do you reach first? Our phone, a person, television, the computer, drugs, alcohol, food and shopping are all possibilities. Sometimes an idol is a habit, person or behavior that isn't good for us, and those are easy to identify. But what about the good things in our life? Our spouses, children, grandchildren, jobs, godly friends, ministry – how can any of those things be an idol? Even good gifts of God can consume our thoughts, control our attention, compete for our affection – and cause us to forget Him. Father uses the word *abandon* in our passage. More than just forgetting to remember – intending to leave. He says further:

"What fault did your ancestors find in me, that they strayed so far from me?" (Jeremiah 2:5)

I am turning my full attention now to anyone who has ever known the pain of being abandoned. I'm not talking about being forgotten, here – I mean *left*. Someone left *you*. Someone purposely chose another. Someone said who you are is not enough for them. This is for the wife of the man who found someone else. For the husband who heard the words, "I don't want to be married anymore." For the parents of the teenager that ran away from home. For the one left at the altar. For the one who knows the sting of unforgiveness from a friend or the rejection from being thought untrustworthy. For the woman who looks in the mirror and sees looking back the scared little girl given away to someone. If you've been abandoned, you know the damage even the most attentive of subsequent spouses, protective parents and faithful friends can't fully repair. For every broken promise that ever broke your heart, you feel deeply the longing from the loving and the leaving.

Wounded Swallow, if I could sit with you right now, I would look right into your sweet eyes and tell you how very sorry I am that you know this devastating sadness. It's pain I know too well myself. To be abandoned *hurts*. It's another person's very intentional decision to leave you, and what it leaves *with* you is a scar that never fully heals. One that, every time the fingertips of your mind run back over it, the jagged edges from the memory resurrects the mantra: "My love is not enough. I am not enough. But someone else *is*." This is sorrow we never forget.

And we inflict this same sorrow on Father every time we choose something or someone over Him.

In the time I described of the busy season in my life, I was serving Jesus and loving it. But it wasn't until the day Holy Spirit spoke something in my heart so clearly it was almost audible that I stopped to really look at my motives. He said, *"You're so busy talking to everyone **about** Me – all I want is for you to just talk **to** Me."* It was then I realized I had begun to crave the affirmation I was receiving from people, rather than approval from God. It breaks my heart to think of Him asking, *"What fault did you find in Me as your source, Loni?"*

Sweetest Swallow, do you feel empty even though your life is full? Do you feel like you're moving from place to place yet going nowhere? Are you restless from seeing God moving in everyone's life while you're struggling? God feels distant – or absent – and you're tired of waiting on Him. Worship is meaningless and mechanical and prayer is repetitive and full of air. Going to church seems pointless and phony so you've stopped going physically or checked out spiritually. When we think God no longer cares, we couldn't care less. When we feel He's not answering, we stop asking. When we believe He let us down, we let Him go. We look back when God was faithful then and wonder why not now? We look now at what's happening to everyone else and wonder *why not me?*

May I lovingly suggest – *perhaps you're drinking from a*

cracked cistern.

God said the second thing His children did was to build for themselves a water source that was damaged and defective. Water was a precious commodity in Jerusalem so the people dug underground receptacles called cisterns outside their homes to hold rainwater. If the water sat too long it became undrinkable – stagnant, stale, cloudy and disease-ridden. If it was cracked, the water would seep out of the sides and leave nothing but mud at the bottom. The unused cistern would be not only be a hindrance, it would be harmful. He used this illustration because His children stopped seeing Him as Provider for their physical and spiritual needs. They aligned themselves with Assyria who had already taken their friends and family hostage, with Babylon who would enslave them later, and with Egypt who had held them captive years before.

You would think once freed, a prisoner would not be so willing to be imprisoned.

The past is the stale waters of a cistern we've built on the foundation of the glory days. The thing about the past is that we either glamorize or dramatize it, but we rarely remember it accurately – drinking from this fountain leaves a sour taste. The present is the muddy waters of the cistern built on self-sufficiency. We can't see clearly and mistakenly rely on our limited knowledge of God's activity in our lives – drinking from this fountain leaves a bitter taste. The future is the cloudy waters of a cistern built on uncertainty. We worry so much with the what-if's of tomorrow that we have no peace today – drinking from this fountain leaves a salty taste. All are disease-ridden waters of the enemy meant to hinder and to harm, to capture and contain, and none can quench the thirst within our souls. If we stay in the past we'll feel stuck in the present and never move ahead to the future. This is how The Counterfeiter traps us! Father is working for our good right now, He has His best for our future, and He has always, always been faithful in our past. Satan wants us to trade the wellspring of water Jesus gives for a flimsy imitation that's his idea of better, but it's a cracked cistern and a copycat convenience. And counterfeit contentment is a cage.

The Hebrew word for swallow is *derowr* – meaning "to move rapidly." Nicknamed "the bird of freedom" because of their swiftness in flight, their love of liberty and speed makes captivity nearly impossible. Looking at this mention of these free birds in Scripture can teach us how to break free:

"Even the sparrow has found a home, and the swallow a nest for herself, where she may have her young – a place near your altar, LORD Almighty, my King and my God." *(Psalm 84:3)*

I love the beauty that the Bird of Freedom, unable to be taken captive, is absolutely captivated by God. These extraordinary creatures will return to the same place year after year to build a home. If you see a nest under the eaves of your church, chances are good it belongs to a swallow. Where The Presence of God inhabits is the one place they can be found, and where they yearn to return. Nearness evokes memory – the closer someone is, we can't forget them. And the more we remain in their presence the more readily we remember.

Sweetest Swallow, if you feel empty, that's a sacred space. That's the deepest place of your heart of hearts yearning to return to The Presence of God. He designed our innermost to recognize and long for Him. In fact, the Hebrew word for "abandon" is the same that God uses in

Genesis 2:24. Just as a man leaves his mother and father to make a dwelling place with his wife, God made our hearts to dwell in His.

---

*If you feel empty, that's the deepest
place of your heart of hearts
yearning to return to
The Presence of God.*

When you feel restless, it's because your heart isn't capable of being at home away from Him. If Father appears distant or absent, press in all the more to His Presence. He wants nothing more than to have your whole heart, because He loves you with all of His. Because of Holy Spirit, we are always in His presence. If there we remain, we won't forget to remember. Like the swallows who return year after year we can make a conscious effort to return to Him day after day.

If your spirit is parched, the best way to quench that thirst is to come directly to the water source. If we drink from a cistern of our own making, we will have to come back again and again. If we depend on our own resources at all, we will come up empty. Christ offers water that will not only satisfy our immediate thirst, we'll never need another source again. He is a free-flowing life spring that bubbles over for all eternity (John 4:13-14). If you're tired of working so hard to overcome cisterns of the past, creating ones right now or concerned for those in the future, lay all that down. You can drink freely from the Living Water that never runs dry. Jesus knows your past and He delivered you from it. He sees your future and has great plans for you. And He is with you in this very moment ready to be your never-ending Spring of Life.

Don't ever settle for a mere drip on the wing, Little Swallow. Stop and drink deeply from The Well.

You will never be abandoned or forgotten by Father (Isaiah 49:15). If we look to Him as our Source, we won't search for another supply. If we watch for Him as our Deliverer, we won't listen to a Deceiver. If we recognize the lies of The Counterfeiter, we'll no longer be a captive.

Beautiful Bird, Jesus came to set you free – and your way

to rescue is about to be revealed.

Chapter Ten: As Free as Bird

"Once you have tasted flight, you will forever walk the earth with your eyes turned skyward, for there you have been, and there you will always long to return."
Leonardo da Vinci

There is a story often used to illustrate freedom I won't likely forget. They say to train a baby elephant, tie one end of a thick rope to his back leg, then secure the other end of the rope to something stationary like a tree or a pole. The little one will immediately pull against the constraint in an effort to break free. He will keep working day after day but will ultimately learn liberty is impossible on his own. His only chance at freedom is release. After a while the young elephant will give up and settle into his captivity, and as time passes what's required to confine him lessens. So much so, eventually a rope is no longer necessary – all that's needed is a simple string. The majestic being with magnificent power within could escape at any time, yet never even tries because he believes for him, freedom is unattainable. Captivity is now comfort to him and his captor – a simple string. This extraordinary creature was meant to live untethered. Unfettered. Undone. He was created to live free.

And so are you.

Come back with me for a moment to the living room. Not to the living room where a little girl had her spiritual identity taken, or to the living room where a grieving sister sat where death and darkness loomed. Today I beckon you to the living room of a young wife and mother who unwittingly accepted a divine invitation to deliverance. While I had already accepted Jesus as my Savior when I was twelve years old, I was yet to know Him as my Lord. I had very limited knowledge of Holy Spirit, and God was anything but Father to me. And, I had *no* idea that He had been orchestrating events even before I was born all to make Himself known. This was the night that changed everything. This was the night I finally knew my name. This was the night I was set free.

A few months prior to that September evening in 1992, a godly woman had been mentoring me. We met in her home as often as we could during lunch, and I listened intently as she gently spoke about God and His love. Over sandwiches and salads, a stony heart was slowly being softened and strongholds were steadily crashing down. One day my friend loaned me a cassette tape of a sermon she'd heard preached in church about the goodness of God. I'm not sure if she will ever really know this side of Heaven what a monumental moment that was, but as she offered the recording, Holy Spirit offered redemption. What I didn't know that night, and what you may not know today is – while salvation for eternity is but once, salvation from ourselves is ongoing. Jesus saves us from the lies we hear from Satan and the lies we tell ourselves.

For almost twenty years I believed the same lie that baby-girl bird from the living room did – since I was unwanted by my biological parents, I was unwanted by everyone – and mostly by God. The Thief held my identity tied by an invisible thread to the inside of a beautiful cage with the door wide open.

What is the lie you've been believing, Beautiful Bird? Have any of the spiritual identity thieves we've talked about been responsible for your restraints? Maybe harmful words spoken to or over you have caused your incarceration. Or you're limping through life fettered to fear. Has malice shackled itself to you? Have you felt the weight from the constraints of comparison? You may be dealing with depression dead-bolted to your heart right this very moment. Or pride has put a padlock on your truth. Or the enslavement of apathy has left you exhausted. You've believed your identity to be that of one who will always be what The Thief has named you. Broken. Ruined. Ashamed. Neglected. Depressed. Insignificant. Empty. Whether one or all, these identity thieves can entrap us only as long as we believe them. Please hear me, though – *they are but flimsy string.* For far too long, the children of God have lived tied up and held hostage by Satan. However, he is only as convincing as his last lie. And he's told his last one today.

This is *your* divine invitation to deliverance.

Do you know that you are so loved, before I could move forward with this chapter, Holy Spirit had me stop right now and pray for *you*? Right now, in this very moment, Father is reaching through time and space today for *you*. This appointment is not happenstance or coincidence. This is a freedom song written for and being sung over *you*, today. No matter who you believe you are, what you've done as a prisoner, where you've been trying to run, when you lost your way, and why you didn't think you're worth it, this is *your* song, Sweetest One. *Can you hear it?*

This is a freedom song written for and being sung over you, today.

The night Father sang over me was quiet, not unlike any other, with my husband at work and my sweet three year old daughter sleeping peacefully down the hall. I listened to the pastor on the recording talk about the goodness of a sovereign God. One who intentionally sought me. One who knew me. One who loved me. *One who wanted me.* In the tiniest of living rooms, I had the greatest of encounters with the living God. He wooed me there. He met me there. He freed me there.

These were the words to my song of redemption:

"The Lord your God is with you, a mighty warrior who saves. He will rejoice over you with gladness. He will quiet you with His love, He will rejoice over you with singing." (*Zephaniah 3:17*)

I wasn't abandoned – *God* was with me. I wasn't unwanted – He *rejoiced* over me. The pastor explained that the word "rejoiced" was not just the feeling of happiness as we know it. No, this was unbridled joy like a parent has over their beloved babies. This was the kind of exuberance that elicits such delight, you can't help but break into song. The preacher said this was not an emotion that anyone on earth could adequately express – this was elation only Father God could possess. And that He was *my* Father.

I have no explanation except that it was supernatural, but I *felt* it – God singing over *me*. The revelation of that truth overwhelmed me with such force, I literally fell on my face in brokenness and gratitude. I don't know how in a space the square footage of a postage stamp, but what felt like the entire presence of the God of the universe permeated the whole of the perimeter of that living room and then knelt down beside me as I drenched the carpet with my sobs. As I lay there, face to the floor weeping, the God I never knew as a father wrapped me in His arms and quieted me with His love. From that quiet collision of grace, He was then and forevermore shall be – *Father*. I speak of Him in first person today because of that *very* personal encounter that night in the living room – the night He gave back my identity. The night He told me I was His.

For the first time, I understood the lengths God had gone to as He played a montage in my mind of all the ways He'd been dropping bread crumbs for me to find throughout my life: by making certain to hand me to a kind man and a generous woman with two nearly-grown boys of their own who loved Jesus more than their own plans for an empty nest and a comfortable life to become my mama and daddy. To choose for me two big brothers to hold and protect my already-fragile heart by not making me feel one time that we didn't share DNA. By making sisters for me with two beautiful women with even more beautiful hearts that married those protectors of mine. To gift me with a husband who cherished me more than his own life and lived it fiercely every day. To allow me the inexpressible privilege of knowing what it meant to have my blood running through someone else's veins with that beautiful sleeping baby girl in the next room with plans for another to come. I had never felt more wanted. The Thief's words of condemnation spoken to an orphaned little girl were systematically being replaced with confident hope. I *did* belong. I wasn't alone and *never* was. I *was* loved. And I *knew* my name that night – *Chosen*.

The background music that was once my lifelong painful soundtrack on repeat now became a beautiful song from my Savior:

Who will I belong to now? Became – *You will always belong to Me.*
I'm all alone in this world. Became – *I never once left your side.*
Will I ever feel safe again? Became – *Your heart is safe with Mine.*

The wailing of my wounded heart was like a battle cry for my Deliverer and He came running. Redemption marched mightily into the cage that night for an identity hanging by a thread. The Mighty Warrior Who Saves instantaneously smashed every single stronghold that had kept me imprisoned for decades and showed me the door for my escape. You see, truth always, always makes way for freedom, and because of it, I believed that I was chosen (Ephesians 1:4), accepted (John 1:12), adopted (Romans 8:15), and redeemed (Colossians 1:13-14). I may have fallen to the floor a frightened baby-girl bird, but know this – I emerged a courageous songbird set free.

Truth always, always makes way for freedom.

The glory of this moment is not mine, however. An important detail you need to know is that *I did not free myself.* This escape was a prison break.

One more look at Psalm 124 explains what I mean. Verses 7-8 talk of the flight from the snare after the harrowing events described in the previous six verses:

We have escaped like a bird from the fowler's snare;
the snare has been broken, and we have escaped.
Our help is in the name of the LORD,
the Maker of heaven and earth.

The snare a fowler used was set with the intention of leading the unsuspecting bird to its death. One method of the hunter was to cover a hole in the ground with leaves. The other was a cage or a trap with bait inside to lure their prey. Whatever prison the bird was placed in was not one they could flee. And like the baby elephant, they soon learned liberty was not possible on their own – the only chance at their freedom would be release.

Satan desires to conceal truth and trap us with lies, but here is reality for you – it doesn't matter if your trap was a hole in the ground of a hunter or you've been caught in the cage of a captor, freedom is yours for the taking. Jesus secured your release when He died for you. He was buried, rose after three days, and today is seated at the right hand of God (1 Corinthians 15:3-4, Romans 8:34). All we have to do is believe to be saved (Acts 16:31). Jesus offers freedom for any captive who will trust Him with their life (Luke 4:18). If you've never trusted in Jesus alone for salvation, today can be your redemption story. Just tell Him you want to be free and then believe in Him to do it.

You may be like me, trusting Jesus as the only way to Heaven, but not trusting Him with day-to-day living. Trying to make it on your own rather than looking to God for help. I had no idea of the power of Holy Spirit that lived within me, so I was existing on my own knowledge and strength and was an easy target for a hunter so shrewd. Is this true for you, too?

Or perhaps you've simply recognized you've been locked in a cage so long you don't know *who* you are – you just know you want to be free.

The weightiness of all of this is not lost on me. I know what it's like to have carried shame and pain and unbelief and fear and doubt so long, you've grown accustomed to them. Holding on to bitterness and anger over past harms and hurts have made you hard. Maybe you've been alone for so long, you've convinced yourself you prefer it. You stare at the wide-open door to your cage, but you believe for you, freedom is unattainable. You never even try to fly, because deep down you don't feel worthy of rescue.

You've been a hostage so long you've lost all hope of release. You take on the chains of the taken identity and succumb to the snare because you don't know how to fly free. You don't think you ever will. Captivity will remain your comfort without a Conqueror.

Your snare has been broken, Sweet Friend. "Broken" in this passage is the Hebrew word *Shabar*. It means to rend violently. To break in or break down. To maim or to cripple. These descriptions are not for the faint of heart. These are war words – indicative of a great battle, of great power and of great defeat. Yet this is not something we can do on our own. Verse seven says we "escaped" but this wasn't a breakout. The word in Hebrew means *to release*. Someone opened the door to the cage, but He doesn't force us out – it's our choice to receive His rescue.

When The Thief took your identity, he waged war with The Warrior Who Saves. If we belong to Jesus, He *is* our identity and we bear His name. And there is such power in that mighty Name! With outstretched arms on an old rugged cross, sin and death and hell and captivity were all crucified with Christ. The snare has been broken and the empty grave is your great escape. This is what it means to be fought *for* – Jesus came right into your captivity and He fought for *you*. He will always fight for you, Little Bird. There is no enemy He can't maim. No cage He can't break. No captive He can't set free.

Do you remember your song?

When a tiny bird enters the world, they don't know how to sing. It's the father that typically teaches his little one the making of a melody. He will croon over his baby bird patiently, continuously, until the music forms an auditory memory of the father's song. Over and over the father sings, just waiting for the day his little one remembers the song he taught them and sings it for themselves. And your heavenly Father sings over you, Sweet Songbird. He sings the song He wrote the day you were created. He sings over you with a beauty that breathes life over the places within that you thought were dead. He sings of freedom and forgiveness and of healing and of help. He sings of redemption and of restoration. He's been singing over you patiently, continuously, as you've read this book – every chapter a chorus, every sentence a sonnet.

In one melodic exchange, your identity has been changed.

You're no longer identified as Broken, Ruined, Ashamed, Neglected, Depressed, Insignificant or Empty. You are now, and forevermore – Beautiful. Royal. Accepted. Noticed. Defended. Important. Embraced.

No matter how your enslavement chapter started, it's not the end of your story. Your rescue was written even before you knew it. Whether you've followed Jesus for years or for seconds, He wants all of you. Every shackle of shame, every fetter of fear – you don't have to bear them any longer. Take everything you know about yourself to everything you know about Father and hand all of it to Him. Lay the very worst and the very best of you before Jesus, and trust Him with your life. He will bring you out of the bondage the enemy placed you in. All He wants is for you to ask Him to.

You were not created for captivity. You are an exquisite, extraordinary creature who was meant to live untethered. Unfettered. Undone. You were meant to live free. My sincerest prayer is that you hear the sweetness of His beautiful voice singing over you as He quiets the sounds of the past with the lyrics of His love. May you remember the song your Father God first sang over you, and sing with

Him today of your deliverance.

So come on out of the cage and fly into freedom, Beautiful Bird. You are a captive no more.